AMERICAN MADE CRISIS:

ALIENS IN OUR MIDST

By

ROY E. PETERSON

TRICROWN BOOKS

American Made Crisis:
Aliens in our Midst

By Roy E. Peterson

Cover Photo Credit: Government Logo

Published on behalf of TriCrown Books by Kindle Direct Publishing, July 2019.

ISBN-9781076282545

Questions: Kindle Publishing or tricrownbooks.com
Available for sale on amazon.com and Kindle.com

FOREWORD

Civil words cannot describe the American made crisis of illegal aliens invading the United States and the short-sighted myopic vision of the American Congress in allowing it to continue unabated over the decades.

Those of the liberal persuasion who now mostly reside in the Democratic Party learned that if illegal aliens also can vote illegally, they will obtain an electoral advantage by keeping the Southern border of the United States open. Perhaps I missed their real intent. It is as though they also favor unfettered entry for drug cartels, violent criminal gangs, sex traffickers, medically unsound, those unable to work and support themselves and dilettantes. Could they profit?

Those of the extremely conservative persuasion have their own agenda of acquiring cheap labor, especially in the construction industry so that illegal aliens can be paid low wages illegally, under the table, and without qualifications or education. $5 an hour is better than $20-$30 and hour.

This American made crisis is a real conspiracy of political expediency by both parties who not only have ignored the problems caused by illegal aliens in our midst, but who continue to obfuscate, circumnavigate, and frustrate the voters and taxpayers of our country causing major economic costs in the trillions (over the decades), subverting the wage bases of American citizens, allowing diseased persons to spread their afflictions among Americans, encouraging social upheaval and moral decay, burdening the American education system and frankly, getting hundreds of Americans killed each year.

The insanity must stop and must stop now. This book will highlight the problem like a neon sign blinking in the face of the intoxicated politically challenged with warnings and dire predictions of the death of our country. Illegal aliens are an American produced tragedy that is a self-inflicted gaping wound.

Roy E. Peterson,
San Angelo, Texas.
July 21, 2019.

TABLE OF CONTENTS

CHAPTER 1

DEFINING THE ILLEGAL ALIEN PROBLEM

Personal Experience with Illegal Aliens

Illegal alien immigration is like rats eating all the corn, wheat and barley in the granary. Soon the farmer can no longer feed the stock or care for his family. Pardon the affrontery, but the parallels are clear between vermin and illegal aliens. I will not resort to the use of rats or vermin for illegal alien terms, but contend that the comparison is both an apt one and applicable in the first two decades of the 21st Century.

Under normal circumstances a nation would declare a crisis, defend its borders from an invasion, and extract or eliminate everyone of the invaders from their country. Apparently America is not a normal country and these are not normal times, rather upsetting ones stirred by insurgents of many varieties on the left and ignored by those who claim Christian compassion for all mankind and those who vacillate politically between left and right. I call these Christians both laissez faire ones and end of the world wishers. Both sides will ruin us.

My first close up and personal experience with the alien/immigration problem was when I flew down to Chula Vista, California in 1986 from Washington, D.C. Another intelligence agent and I flew an evening border patrol out of Brown Field and surveyed the border crossers. I wanted to call them neither immigrants or aliens at the time, but criminal offenders or invaders. Immigrants are invited guests awaiting citizenship processing. Aliens are offenders of law and order.

Yes, some are good and nice; however, the real criminals in their presence makes any of them unacceptable, unwanted, undocumented and undesirable.

I was struck by the crowds waiting until evening on the Mexican side of the border and then as dusk approached began streaming over light obstacles into the United States.

The entire border came alive with action as most of the invaders were rounded up by helicopter, ATV's, pickups, and Jeeps. They were herded into canyons and other dead-end locations, caught, put into buses and placed in detention facilities at San Ysidro. At least those who were caught. Some of them were trying for their umpteenth time.

I was angry then at the onslaught; the brazen running and jumping across the border in plain sight. I am even more angry now, but with presidents prior to President Trump and also with Congress, then and especially now, for not having solved the problem and allowing it to continue.

Border ranchers have been complaining about the invasion of the illegal aliens on their ranches since the 1980's. Prior to that time they were mostly friendly and quiet, not wanting to attract attention and moving on quickly without bothering the rancher or his family. Now they are in mortal danger.

As an intelligence operative, I knew we were catching infiltrators then from the Communist bloc and China at the Mexican border. Since this was the 1980's, we also had unwelcome guest from Soviet satellite countries like Poland and the Czech Republic. I was the Executive Officer of an Intelligence Company and an agent who I supervised spent considerable time on call at the detention facility to debrief those from countries other than Mexico.

There are road warning signs between San Diego and the highway checkpoint near Camp Pendleton that show a running family and words to beware fleeing persons. The necessity for such signs was back in the 1990's and on my last drive up Interstate 5 in 20010, the signs were still there.

Later in my life on my way from Arizona and my home in 2006 to my company headquarters early one morning at zero dark thirty, I missed what I believe was alien running across the road as I approached Indio. When I realized I missed, I felt it could not have been more than four feet. I had my car set at exactly the speed limit of 70 mph and had no time to react. I had to take a few deep breaths on that one and then wondered how much damage it would have caused to my Lincoln Town Car. The fleeting figure had on a purple robe, but I knew instantly it was not a priest or a monk.

Illegal Aliens, Illegal Immigrants and Other Terms

To have a civil discussion about the American made crisis, we first need to agree on the term for the invaders. The term "rats" and "trash" do not encourage a dispassionate debate, even though they may be the most appropriate ones in this case.

"Wetbacks" is an old term used for this group, since they often were considered to have swum across the Rio Grande River; however, there are portions of the border where simply walking across is sufficient without a water obstacle between them and the United States. They were the former agricultural workers allowed to be in fields in at least the southern part of the United States from California's orchards and San Joaquin vegetable farms to the cotton farms of south and west Texas.

I will refer to the official name of "Operation Wetback" later when I discuss a current program aimed at sending them back to Mexico.

"Undocumented immigrants," or "undocumented aliens" are the softer terms often employed in polite discourse. Those are politically correct, yet grossly incorrect and inadequate terms. I will use the term "illegal aliens" as the most accurate acceptable term. I do so though with an explanation of the linkage of illegal with alien and with immigrant. Undocumented is meant to cut out what some consider the pejorative use of illegal; however, I will call it by the name in reality and in our laws.

There is a distinction between aliens and immigrants. Aliens are non-citizens and non-nationals who go to another country usually to live for a specified period of time such as on a work visa permit. Immigrants are aliens who have been granted the right to reside permanently in another country. Aliens do not have permanent resident status and no expectation of that status unless they later convert their visas and apply for citizenship by chance or trickery.

Immigrants enter a country for the express purpose of residing permanently in that country. Legal immigrants are given visas in various categories for that purpose. Example of aliens are foreign students, foreign workers, specified non-permanent residence persons, and corporate personnel present in country for a specific purpose.

An immigrant is foreign born, but has been accorded permanent residence of a country. Illegal aliens have no status granted by anyone to enter a country, live off the proceeds of that country, and in effect steal resources of a country. They are just that – illegal!

Differences between Illegal Aliens/Immigrants and Legal Immigrants

Since all non-native Americans identify themselves as having come from immigrant stock, the average American has no discernment of the differences and many erroneously have empathy or hate for anyone labelled an immigrant. This deceptive falsehood is perpetuated by the native Americans who view all immigrants as illegal, thus lumping the non-native population into one class. I assure you the difference is vast and it is not a difference of degree, but of kind.

This is highly significant for Americans. It is the difference between accepting those with the greatest disposition toward being law-abiding, self-providing contributors to American civilized life and those with the strongest possible propensity toward violence including rape and murder of real American citizens.

The three most important differences are: 1.) Medical and physical checkups by approved doctors, 2.) Security checks with local and national agencies in the country of origin, and 3.) Proof of means (financial support):

1. Medical checks. Medical checkups are an important part of legal immigration and they are conducted by doctors in the other country and checked by medical personnel assigned or trusted by American Embassies or Consulates in those countries of origin.

In Moscow in the 1970's, the Swiss had a medical facility that often was used for the purpose of completing medical paperwork for a visa to the United States of any category. They also had a dental clinic operated by a beautiful female dentist who they imported from Hungary.

2. Security checks. Vetting is part of the process to acquire background information on the good citizens versus criminal citizens as categorized by the country from which immigrants are allowed access as visitors, guest workers, or those who are seeking permanent residence and citizenship. Without the vetting that includes criminal background reports and interviews, a country invites disaster and corruption.

3. Proof of Means. A third important review is one for proof of means, which is intended to insure survival without welfare in the United States. Proof of means may be provided by a friend or relative sponsor, either one who will take them into their home. A work sponsor guarantees work for the time stamped on their visa up to five years. A student visa is another visa category that proves means and sustainability.

The tests for citizenship and literacy are important for confirming ability to process information and to become acculturated citizens who respect things like the meaning of the flag and the Pledge of Allegiance. This oath is an important psychological underpinning for a new citizen.

The following table provides a descriptive comparison of the majority of those differences between legal immigrants and illegal aliens. The distinctions are of vital importance and graphically show why it is so important for our present debate in 2019 and into the future to understand what is at stake.

Table 1-1

LEGAL IMMIGRANTS VERSUS ILLEGAL ALIENS

LEGAL IMMIGRANTS	ILLEGAL ALIENS
Medical Checkups both prior to visa and at the immigration station reduces to almost zero the potential for carrying a disease to the US.	No medical checkups means untreated, unmitigated personal transportation of devastating foreign diseases.
Criminal Background checks for drugs, sex trafficking, homicides, robberies, and other crimes greatly reduce likelihood of criminal behavior in the United States.	No criminal background checks means many illegals were and may still be criminals greatly increasing the odds of continued criminal enterprise in the US.
Must pass **means test** so as not to become a potential burden for the US taxpayer.	No means test indicates future reliance on US welfare system at taxpayer expense.
Must pass a **test for citizenship and for literacy** This means they have minimal understanding what it means to be an American and the ability to read and write as a partial literacy test.	No test means no effort to teach American government, history and values. Nothing to show they are capable of learning and adjusting to America.
No basis for blackmail and exploitation in the US as an illegal immigrant.	Complete basis for blackmail and exploitation in the US as an illegal immigrant and fear of reporting crime.
Stated oath and intention to abide by US law.	No stated intention to abide by US law.
Entitled to citizenship benefits.	Not entitled to citizenship benefits.

In each of the seven (7) boxes for legal immigrants, I highlighted the positive characteristics and entitlements that powerfully connote the difference between being a legal immigrant and an illegal alien. They are not the same. A legal citizen belongs. An illegal alien does not! I pray you see and embrace the gulf between the two while paying particular attention to the used of the word, "immigrant."

Deportation Versus Repatriation

The words, "deportation" and "repatriation" have radically opposite connotations with deportation being the negative one and repatriation being the positive one. Debates are won or lost in Congress and with the American people over the use of these terms and branding the American consciousness.

Deportation is widely associated with those engaged in criminal behavior, those who are illegally present in the United States and those assessed as not being worthy of American citizenship such as traitors and those who acquired citizenship through illegal or corrupt means.

Repatriation sounds like a term signaling those who wish to voluntarily return to their country or origin, whether they do or not. Repatriation can be considered a term of respect with the American immigration system helping them to get back to where they belong and wish to be.

Words are important in winning debates. Politicians would do well to pay attention to the connotation of the use of these words.

A Look Ahead to Chapter 2

When I began this book, I did not intend to spend much time on the history and patterns of immigration. As I began my writing, I realized the importance of setting down historical milestones. I succumbed to the Historian and Political Scientist that I have been, but more than that, the arguments now being presented both to the American people and to the Supreme Court in 2019, such as placing the citizenship status question on the Census 2020 forms, require attorneys, historians, political scientists, demographers, and others engaged in debate to use and understand precedent and the historical perspective.

CHAPTER 2

IMMIGRATION HISTORY AND PATTERNS

Historical Overview of Immigration to the United States 1790-1850

With civilization and government, come order and enhanced population protection as the first basic necessity for survival. Orderly national immigration to the United States first was ordained by President Benjamin Harrison in 1890, when he took control of future immigration anywhere in the United States, but primarily from Europe. President Harrison designated Ellis Island as the immigration processing station. Ellis Island station opened January 1, 1892 with the mandate to ensure no more indentured servants were being brought to the United States from Europe, no criminals from those countries entered, and all were medically sound.

Prior to the opening of Ellis Island for national immigration control in 1890, the states were responsible for immigration acceptance, incarceration, or deportation. As you can imagine, sometimes deportation meant to a neighboring state.

Immigrants were normally processed with proper documentation such as a birth certificate and passport reasonably quickly with some delayed up to five hours. Those arriving first and second class on vessels were allowed quicker entry because it was deemed they could afford the passage and were more worthy of acceptance. Many though were detained overnight in dormitories set up for the purpose of temporary housing. Those arriving third class were checked more thoroughly and often stayed overnight in dormitories established for temporary lodging.[1]

Later immigrants had to have a passport, visa, and had to pass a literacy test. In the meantime the Mexican and the Canadian borders remained a sieve.

Date and place of birth has always been an integral part of the immigration documentation and is an important statement on all census documentation. That means the documentation in a census year can be checked back to what is placed on the form and discrepancies now with computer assistance can compare those who lie about the location and can point to suspected illegal immigrants regardless of whether the citizenship question is on the census agenda. Thus they can be discounted from the roles of citizenship!

From the Mayflower to the establishment of the United States of America, the populations of the colonies were made up 90% of natural birth population growth. Immigration rarely exceeded 10% with the last colonies experiencing significant immigration being North and South Carolina, largely from England and Scotland, followed by Pennsylvania with a large Germanic contingent. In the other colonies growth mainly came from internal migration and natural birth increasesd as the populations expanded to new and opening lands further west.[2]

Surprisingly, over half of the British immigrants in the southern colonies came as indentured servants primarily poor young people who could not find work in England or other countries of the British Isles and came bound by their future masters who paid for their passage across the Atlantic Ocean.

Besides this number, approximately 60,000 British convicts were transported in the 1700's to the British colonies until the establishment of the United States, at which time they often were sent to Australia and New Zealand, which were identified largely as penal colonies until the early 1900's.

The first penal colony there was established in 1788 at

New South Wales at Botany Bay.[3]

Transport of convicts both to the American colonies and to the Australian/New Zealand ones was chaining below deck as African slaves had been. In neither case were most of them hardened criminals, but those like a 70-year-old woman who stole some cheese to eat. They were simply guilty of being out of work and poor. On the other hand, the peers in England considered all convicts as incapable of rehabilitation. Those who committed heinous crimes were executed, the rest were banished to the colonies.

It may seem strange, but these were the only immigrants with the most complete immigration records. Others simply showed up with few or no records.[4]

The United States Census was mandated by the Constitution of the United States every ten years by Article 1, Section 2 which stipulates, "Representatives and direct Taxes shall be apportioned among the several States...according to their respective numbers...The actual Enumeration shall be made within three Years after the first meeting of the Congress of the United States, and within every subsequent Term of Ten years." Section 2 further specifies Representatives shall be apportioned among the several States according to their respective number, counting the whole number of persons in each State...excluding Indians..."[5]

The first census was taken in 1790 under the direction of then Secretary of State, Thomas Jefferson.[6]

By 1830 more complete records of immigration were kept than before. Many of the previous estimates come from ship logs and passenger lists.

Although immigration records were spotty up to 1850, a check of available records indicate "immigration totaled 8,385 in the year of 1820, with immigration totals gradually increasing to 23,322 by the year 1830; for the 1820's decade ,immigration more than doubled to 143,000."[7]

"Between 1831 and 1840, immigration more than quadrupled to a total of 599,000.....Between 1841 and 1850, immigration nearly tripled again, totaling 1,713,000 immigrants, including at least 781,000 Irish, 435,000 Germans, 267,000 British, and 77,000 French."[8]

The Irish Potato Famine of 1845 to 1848 led families to escape poverty and death, while the failed revolutions of 1845 and 1848 brought the intellectuals and activists from Europe. [8]

Table 2-1

CENSUS OF THE U.S. POPULATION 1790-1850

Census Date	Population	Immigrants By Decade
1790	3,918,000	60,000
1800	5,236,000	60,000
1810	7,036,000	60,000
1820	10,086,000	60,000
1830	12,785,000	143,000
1840	17,018,000	599,000
1850	23,054,000	1,713,000

Note: Immigrants 1790-1820 are estimates.
Source: U.S. Census Bureau.[9]

1850 marked the first-time place of birth was specifically asked, setting a precedent for the question of citizen or noncitizen. With the Treaty concluding the Mexican War in 1848, part of the immigrant increase from 1840 to 1850 was due to the US extending citizenship to approximately 60,000 Mexican residents in New Mexico Territory and 10,000 more living in California.

The California gold rush attracted 100,000 potential miners or miner support persons from the Eastern US, Latin America, China, Australia and Europe.[10] This allowed California to apply for statehood in 1850.

Historical Overview of Immigration to the United States1851-1950

From my studies, one of the largest increases in U.S. population throughout the 1800's was the addition of states to the Union. This included everyone in Texas (1846) and California (1850). California was the 31st state added to the Union, so one can begin to grasp the additional numbers added by statehood throughout that century and into the early 1900's with the additions of Oklahoma and Arizona.

Hawaii and Alaska were the final two adding gross numbers of population. Although this is a prominent statistic, many of the sources tend to discuss from where immigrants came and forget to simply add the new populations.

Many of the states relied on federal census data conducted by territorial Governors to apply for admission to the Union. Others had to conduct a census as part of the statehood application process. According to the Northwest Ordinance of 1787, a territory applying to become a state was required to have 60,000 population.

Some territorial legislatures began the application process below that number in anticipation of having 60,000 population by the time of consideration. They conducted a supplemental census during the process. Some had a sudden boost in population just by advertising they were applying for statehood, such as Ohio and Indiana. While their numbers might have been suspect, within the next ten years they tripled and quadrupled in size making any challenges moot.

Data for the following Table 2-3, "Population of States at Time of Entry (1803-1959) was acquired from a number of sources including U.S. Census Bureau, claims by the territories, and territorial records. I did not find one chart for all of them and had to make the composite table (Table 3 below).

The Northwest Ordinance requirement for 60,000 population apparently was a flexible one, especially in the case of Nevada, which had an exceptionally low threshold number of only 10,000.

Table 2-2

Population of States at Time of Entry (1803-1959)

#	Year	State	Population Added to U.S.	Notes
17	1803	Ohio	60,000	45,365 in 1800 census
18	1812	Louisiana	76,556	As of 1810 census
19	1816	Indiana	60,000	24,520 in 1810 census
20	1817	Mississippi	100,000	½ of Miss. Territory
21	1818	Illinois	60,000	40,278 in 1st 1818 census
22	1819	Alabama	100,000	½ of Miss. Territory
23	1820	Maine	298.335	1820 census
24	1821	Missouri	66,586	1820 census
25	1836	Arkansas	60,000	52,240 in 1835 census
26	1837	Michigan	87,000	1837 census
27	1845	Florida	70,966	1845 census
28	1845	Texas	125,000	Census plus estimate
29	1846	Iowa	80,000	Census plus estimate
30	1848	Wisconsin	300,000	Census plus estimate
31	1850	California	92,597	1850 census
32	1858	Minnesota	157,000	As of 1857
33	1859	Oregon	52,465	1860 census
34	1861	Kansas	107,206	1860 census
35	1863	W. Virginia	376,688	1860 census
36	1864	Nevada	10,000	6,857 1860 census[3-1 Note]
37	1867	Nebraska	60,000	122,993 in 1870 census
38	1876	Colorado	60,000	194,327 in 1880 census
39	1889	N, Dakota	151,500	1885 census for North half
40	1889	S. Dakota	348,600	1890 census
41	1889	Montana	142,924	1890 census
42	1889	Washington	357,232	1890 census
43	1890	Idaho	88,548	1890 census
44	1890	Wyoming	60,705	1890 census
45	1896	Utah	276,479	By end of the century data
46	1907	Oklahoma	1,414,771	As stated.
47	1912	New Mexico	327,301	1910 census
48	1912	Arizona	204,354	1910 census
49	1959	Hawaii	632,772	1960 census
50	1959	Alaska	226,167	1960 census

3-1 Note: Nevada expanded to 42,000 by the 1870 census, but the usual 60,000 population size was waived, partly because of the silver mines.

I understand the reluctance to tackle this murky population addition problem. The addition of these states was not a concomitant addition to the overall U.S. population as they gained statehood, since a large number of them were U.S. citizens already. Emigrants from other countries and children of U.S. citizens moving to territories; however, had not been counted previously. For example, one of my grandfathers was born in Dakota Territory in 1886 before South Dakota became a state. This actually held up my own security clearance initially, since the reviewer thought that meant foreign-born.

My point is that a certain percentage of the population of the new states admitted to the Union were indeed increases to the overall net population of the United States with the exceptions of at least Hawaii and Alaska which were already counted.

Immigration between the census years of 1850 and 1950 is largely attributable to events in Europe and the changes in fortune of those coming to America.

German Immigration

Approximately 5 million Germans migrated to the United States in the century between 1850 and 1950, settling primarily in the Midwest with some in Texas and some connecting with relatives in places like Pennsylvania. Many of them were skilled workers and were employed in industrial factories. 170,000 German immigrants joined the Union Army.[11]

British and Irish Immigration

3.5 million British settled in the United States during this century span with many of them adapting to the cities in the East and Midwest.

The British numbers were a million less than the 4.5

million Irish who entered America. Prior to 1845, the Irish immigrants were largely Protestant. After 1845, the Irish were mainly Catholic. The years 1845-1849 marked the zenith of the potato famine in Ireland caused by a disease called simply, "the blight," or "late blight."[12]

During the Civil War, 140,000 Irish by place of birth joined the Union Army.[12] Many of this group made up the indentured servants until after the Civil War, since the blight wiped out their farms and they were left essentially destitute. The Irish were sold just like slaves in markets in Britain, bought by land owners needing field workers and domestics, and transported the same way as the African slaves had been, that is, tied down and shackled below deck.

Eastern and Southern European Immigration

Four factors may be cited for the increasing numbers of immigrants from Eastern Europe and Southern Europe:

1. Mechanization of farming equipment contributed to a labor surplus, especially among the younger set.
2. Expansion of European railroads, especially connecting port cities with boats and ship, meant cheap tickets and ease of access to the ports and ships for lower classes.
3. Larger steam-powered ships meant reduced ticket costs that could be afforded by lower classes.
4. Continuing political instability through the regions.

This is often called the third wave of immigration. Young people ages 15-30 predominated. Some termed this wave a "flood" of immigrants with 25 million from Slavic countries like Russia, Poland and Hungary along with Italians and Greeks.

Prominent among the "Russians" were the Volga Germans, who had been invited to farm free land under

Catherine the Great, but who now were people without a country and without the backing of the government of Russia. The name came from their concentration in the southern Volga agricultural region. With the timing of arrival after 1880, large numbers responded to newspaper adds in the east for homesteading the newly opened free lands in the Dakotas and Nebraska.

Mixed in with these immigrants, especially from Eastern Europe Slavic countries and the Hapsburg Empire, were up to four (4) million Jews who fled pograms of the 1800's, especially in Austria. Jewish immigration then increased during the 1930s with the ascendancy of Hitler and the Nazi Party to power. Many of these sought asylum in the United States and elsewhere, such as the United Kingdom.

French Canadian Immigration

Immigration directly from France was always low and the primary destination over the century was Louisiana; however, immigration of French Canadians from Quebec, Canada was highly disproportionate to the numbers living there. Between 1840 and 1950, 900,000 French Canadians immigrated to the United States with the concentration in New England.[15]

The Acadians settled in what was once termed New France that extended from the Eastern Canadian Maritime provinces of Nova Scotia, New Brunswick and Prince Edward Island down to the Kennebec River in Maine. They immigrated largely from the coastline of France to the Maritime provinces in the 17th and 18th centuries. A significant number of them were deported from France, or fled France after the European revolutions from 1845 and 1848. Cajuns were the Louisiana counterpart of these deportations and voluntary flights.

Immigration Patterns and Laws 1843-1949

The first federal government immigration law was passed in 1875 as a reaction to a U.S. Supreme Court ruling that states did not have the authority to pass legislation restricting immigration to the United States. Prior to the Page Act of 1875, several groups, often called xenophobic ones, attempted to pressure state legislatures to curb immigration of various kinds and from various nations. These groups gained some momentum just prior to and then after the Civil War.

1843-1856: Anti-Catholic Immigration Effort.

A wave of anti-Catholic immigrant sentiment in New England, especially in New York, led to the loose formation of groups to pressure Congress to quell immigration from the Catholic areas of Ireland, but their efforts were overtaken by antislavery causes and nothing came of the effort.

A party was formed with the express purpose of stopping Catholic immigration, but it faded with the Civil War, because of the new need for workers to replace the ones now in the Union Army and because of the sentiments against slavery and the political battles of the fours or so prior to the war.

1875 Supreme Court Ruling.

In the American west, Chinese laborers and Asian prostitutes were imported; the laborers to work on the western portions of the new cross-country railroads and prostitutes to satisfy the wants and needs of all the single men attracted to the gold mines and other western enterprises.

In the Eastern United States, Irish provided most of the new slave labor both for railroad construction and for their brawn in working in coal mines as they had done in Ireland.

In the case of <u>Chy Lung v. Freeman</u> 92 U.S. 275 (1875) the Supreme Court of the United States unanimously ruled in favor of Chy Lung whose attorney made the primary argument that the State of California did not have the authority to impose restrictions on Chinese immigration. Only the U.S. Federal Government had the authority to impose any restrictions, thus Chy Lung, a Chinese immigrant, could immigrate to California without any restrictions being imposed. Prior to that time every state made their own restrictive or non-restrictive laws.[14]

1875 Nation's First Immigration Law, the Page Act

Reacting to the Supreme Court ruling on the Chy Lung case, Congress passed the first immigration law under the Page Act of 1875. This act is known as the "Asian Exclusion Act," although it further prohibited immigration of those convicted of crimes in other countries.

The Act specifically outlawed importation of Asian contract laborers, Asian women who planned to engage in prostitution, and those from all countries who were convicts in their native land.[15]

1882 Chinese Exclusion Act

The Page Act was followed up specifically by the "Chinese Exclusion Act" preventing all Chinese laborers from entering the country for a period of ten years. The law was renewed in 1892 and 1902; however, Chinese migrants illegally entered the United States crossing the loosely guarded U.S.-Canadian border.[16]

1890's.

The 1890's portended further restrictions on

immigration, or at least control of the process. These events can quickly be summarized as:

1. The Immigration Act of 1891 established a Commissioner of Immigration under the U.S. Treasury Department.

2. Formation of the Immigration Restriction League was in 1894 in Boston.

3. The Canadian Agreement of 1894 primarily resulted in extending U.S. immigration restrictions to Canadian ports, where those restricted by U.S. law could be prevented from leaving for destinations in the United States. The Canadian Agreement is significant as a precedent for agreement with Mexico to prevent illegal immigration of aliens to the United States after 2016.[17] (History)

1907 Dillingham Commission

The Dillingham Commission was established by Congress in 1907 for the purpose of investigating the overall effects of immigration on the United States. A massive 40-volume analysis with considerable statistical data was produced covering the previous three decades.

The main conclusion of the Dillingham Commission was immigration patterns shifted from Central, Northern and Western Europe to Southern Europe and Russia.[18]

1917 Literacy Requirement

Immigration activists in the United States lobbied since the mid-1800's to enforce a literacy requirement on those seeking citizenship in the United States. The interesting thing about effort was it centered on a literacy test in their native language as a measure to test their intellectual capacity, not on their use of English to enter the United States, which would have been highly restrictive.

New immigrants were feared to lack political, social and occupational skills in order to become productive members of society and assimilate into American culture.

The big question: **Was America still a melting pot or had it become a dumping ground?**

Congress considered the argument of the great majority of immigrants being poor and without education and passed a new immigration act to quell the "surge of lower-class immigrants from Southern and Eastern Europe."[19] The League managed to get Congress to pass a similar literacy bill in 1897, but it was vetoed by President Grover Cleveland; however, in 1917, Congress passed an even more restrictive version and then passed it with two-thirds majority over the veto of then President Woodrow Wilson. [20]

1921 Emergency Quota Act

The most important legislation from the early twentieth century came in 1921. Referred to as the 1921 Quota Act, this legislation utilized immigration statistics to determine a maximum number of immigrants allowed to enter the United States from each nation or region. The numbers were skewed to favor immigration from western European nations while severely curbing immigration from areas perceived to be undesirable.

The quotas were set on certain permissible percentage. For the Asians no more than 2% of the levels of nationalities as represented in the 1890 census were allowed to immigrate to the United States. This resulted in the effective banning of all Asian immigration.[20]

A push was on for immigrants to enter other ports, particularly Galveston and San Francisco. This led to some changes in the 1921 law.

1924 Immigration Law

As presented in <u>History.com</u>, "Subsequent immigration to the United States sharply declined, and, in 1924 a law was passed requiring immigrant inspection in countries of origin, leading to the closure of Ellis Island and other major immigrant processing centers (such as those in Galveston and on the West Coast). Between 1892 and 1924, some 16 million people successfully immigrated to the United States..."[21]

The national origins formula of 1921 and codification in 1924 excluded all immigrants from elsewhere in the Western Hemisphere from the quota system allowing free movement from Mexico, the Caribbean nations and the rest of Central and South America.

The application of the 1924 law lasted until 1965, but there were exceptions made to the rule for emergency purposes. These considerations for special treatment and access with proper vetting, of course, included:

1. Jewish refugees from Nazi Germany before WWII and after the Second World War for survivors of the Holocaust.

2. Non-Jewish displaced persons escaping Communist rule in Central Europe and the Soviet Union.

3. Hungarians seeking refuge after suppression of their uprising in 1956.

4. Cubans after the 1960 Castro Communist revolution in 1960.

5. Foreign application by males to join the United States military as soldiers and achieve citizenship as promised to them at the time.

1934 Equal Nationality Act

The Equal Nationality Act allowed children born abroad of American mothers, but with alien fathers who entered the U.S. before the age of 18 and who lived in the U.S. for five years to apply for American citizenship; made the process of naturalization quicker and easier for alien husbands of American citizen wives; and equalized expatriation, immigration, naturalization, and repatriation between women and men. It did not apply retroactively, but was modified by later laws such as the Nationality Act of 1940.[22]

1934 Tydings-McDuffie Act

The Tydings-McDuffie Act of 1934 gave independence to the Philippines, though the date was forwarded to July 4, 1946. The Act maintained the restrictive Asian formula effectively limiting immigration from there to the United States until the law was revised in 1965.[23] Many of the Filipino entrants in the late 1940s were women married to American servicemen and came under the War Brides Act of 1945.

Post-War Operation Paperclip

Operation Paperclip was the effort to identify and locate the great rocket and jet scientists or those of intellectual value from the former Third Reich and get them to safety in America, largely in West Texas and New Mexico. These scientists and intellectuals were admitted through intelligence channels and provided highly significant invaluable resources for the military and eventually space programs with Werner Von Braun the obvious most important of these.

There were complaints of former Nazis among them, but science and invention were paramount. Besides every German could have been a Nazi Party member.

1945 War Brides Act

The War Brides Act of 1945 allowed the foreign-born wives of American servicemen to immigrate to the United States and in 1946 was amended to allow fiancées of American servicemen to migrate, as well.[24]

1946 Luce-Celler Act

The Luce-Celler Act further extended the right to become naturalized citizens to Filipinos from the newly independent Philippines and to Asian Indians; however, the number was set at 100 per year per country.[25]

1948 Displaced Persons Act

The first Displaced Persons Act was signed by President Truman in 1948. This first displacement Act set aside some of the quotas for Europeans, included a provision for orphans of war and gave regular status to thousands already in the United States as of 1948. While Asians were not included in setting aside of quotas, the Act gave permanent residence to many Chinese already residing in the United States. 200,000 displaced persons were allowed entry with permanent status under this act.[26]

Summary of Changes 1843 to 1949

The biggest change to immigration came with the Supreme Court Case of Chy Lung v. Freeman in 1875, when the Supreme Court took immigration laws and control from the states and mandated the federal government be in complete control. The Page Act of 1875, immediately gave the responsibility to the U.S. Treasury Department. Various methods of controlling immigration led to the quota system specifying the numbers that could come from each country and excluding those of others.

The war years of the two world wars put a damper on immigration. After the Second World War, Congress and the President took pity on displaced persons and other categories of immigrants. Congress passed legislation to provide broader access on a temporary basis to these groups.

Immigration Patterns and Laws 1950 to 2000

After World War II, normalization of immigration rapidly filled the national origins quotas from war torn Europe. Between 1941 and 1950, 1,035,000 people immigrated to the U.S.[27]

Second Displaced Persons Act of 1950

The second Displaced Person Act permitted entry for another 200,000-person displaced by the war and included entry for permanent residence to common German families, such as those engaged in agriculture as long as they had sponsorship. 55,000 of them were included in the 200,000. Families for sponsorship were found by charitable organizations like the Lutheran World Federation and other ethnic and religiously affiliated groups.[28]

1950 Internal Security Act

After the Korean War broke out in 1950, Congress passed the Internal Security Act. This Act barred admission of Communists in particular, since they might engage in activities "which could be prejudicial to the public interest, or would endanger the welfare or safety of the United States."[29]

Third Displaced Persons Act of 1953

The third Displaced Persons Act of 1953, brought laborers and agricultural workers to supplant servicemen returned to duty for the Korean War. Another 200,000 were allowed outside the overall quota system and over subsequent years a total of nearly 600,000 refugees and orphans were allowed entry to the United States. This was second only to 650,000 Jews, many of whom were fleeing Communist takeovers of Central European nations.[30]

On a personal note, I remember the Wesselman farm family near Bonesteel, South Dakota, sponsored the Schoenhof family from Germany. Klaus, Crystal and Margaret Schoenhof were dropped into our school system in 1954. Klaus and Crystal were placed in Bonesteel High School and Margaret was a grade ahead of me in the eighth grade. I particularly remember Margaret, because she loved to play basketball after school with me. My mother was a teacher and often spent an extra hour grading papers and preparing for the next day of classes. In my seventh-grade class was Carol Brunner, whose family was sponsored. Her father established the first television sales and maintenance store in Bonesteel.

1952 Immigration and Nationality Act (McCarran-Walter Act)

Over much Congressional debate and the opposition of President Truman to the basis for immigration being reaffirmed as the nation-of-origin quota system of 1924, the McCarran-Walter Act, as it often is called, passed over the veto of President Truman.

While the Act ended Asian exclusion, it further "introduced a system of preferences based on skill sets and family reunification."[31]

The central concern of the policy was national security and vetting immigrants prior to arrival. Democratic Congressman,

Emanuel Celler of New York, favored liberalization of immigration laws favoring Northern Europe to the rest of the world contending that it created resentment in third world countries and Eastern Europe.

Pat McCarran, on the other hand, the Democratic Senator from Nevada, worked with Democratic Congressman from Pennsylvania, Francis Walter, to hammer out the final Act demonstrating the fear of communist infiltration through immigration and the belief that unassimilated aliens could threaten the foundations of American life. Preservation of national security and the national interest thus gained ascendancy and overall Congressional approval.[32]

Revision was made to the 1924 formula to allow for one-sixth of one percent of each nationality's population in the United States as of 1920. This meant 85% of the 154,277 visas available annually were allotted to those of northern and western European heritage. It further continued deletion of Western Hemisphere countries from the quota system, although it did introduce a new period of residency requirement to quality for quota-free entry.[33]

A minimum quota of 100 visas per year was allotted each Asian nation and restriction were eliminated preventing Asians from becoming naturalized citizens. The new law was based on Asian race instead of nationality. Thus, an individual with one or more Asian parents who was born anywhere in the world and possessed citizenship of any nation was counted under the Asian ethnicity quota.[34]

A system of priority preferences was provided American consuls in American Embassies and Consulates favoring special skills and/or families already resident in the United States. The Act further gave non-quota status to alien husbands of American citizens. Wives had been entering outside the quota system for several years by 1952. A labor certification was also established to prevent new immigrants from becoming unwanted competition for American laborers.[35]

1953 Refugee Relief Act

President Dwight D. Eisenhower signed the Refugee Relief Act of 1953 into law. The need was to replace the Displaced Persons Act of 1948 which expired at the end of 1952. Initially labelled the Emergency Migration Act, the bill was written at the request of President Eisenhower to admit more immigrants from Southern Europe.

McCarran again was the chief architect of the bill as he had been on the 1952 legislation, but in the end did not vote in favor, although it was passed. The results of the legislation were the admission of 214,000 immigrants to the United States outside the quota system of the 1952 bill and included 60,000 Italians, 17,000 Greeks, 17,000 Dutch, and 45,000 from countries under Communist control.[36]

Of particular note, amendments required applicants to undergo an in-depth security screening with a verifiable history of their most recent activities in the two years prior to application. The bill cleared the House by a vote of 221 to 185 with the support of most of the Democrats and an even Republican split. It passed the Senate on a voice vote.

McCarran publicized his opposition claiming "We have in the United States today hard-core, indigestible blocs which have not become integrated into the American way of life, but which, on the contrary are its deadly enemies."[36]

Refugees were defined as immigrants who lacked "the essentials of life." That is why in order to become eligible, refugees had the requirement to find an American sponsor who would guarantee them a home and a job.

Italian and Greek Americans were permitted apply for their relatives to be admitted above the standing refugee quota level.[36]

1954 "Operation Wetback"

The bracero program that allowed Mexican workers to come to the states as **"temporary"** agricultural workers during and after World War II as necessary manpower was sometimes referred to as "the decade of the wetback." Estimates are that prior to the program forcing them to return to Mexico, more than a million workers crossed the Rio Grande illegally. The term, "wetback," refers to illegal swimming across the border via the Rio Grande.

After the war, this cheap labor was found to be displacing native agricultural workers, violated labor laws, encouraged criminals, brought diseases such as tuberculosis, and presented a large number of illiterates. This should sound familiar to present day public health officials and doctors serving the Border Patrol needs.

The President's (Truman) Commission on Migratory Labor in Texas reported cotton growers in Texas and the Rio Grande Valley paid migrant field workers approximately half the wages paid elsewhere in Texas for similar agricultural work. The Border Patrol was then tasked under the Eisenhower Administration in 1954 to enlist the assistant of municipal, county, state, and federal authorities to remove the Mexican citizens working in Texas.

The military was added to the effort making it a quasi-military operation. By announcing the roundup as Operation Wetback, the government hoped to force most of them to flee the country. Many did in fact leave voluntarily. The Immigration and Naturalization Service claimed by end of the operation they removed as many as 1,300,000, although the number did not match the much lower numbers apprehended.

The program was abandoned over questions about ethics in implementation of the operation and accusations of "police-state methods."[37]

1956-1960 Hungarian Revolution Refugees

Before the Soviet Union decided to crush the Hungarian Revolution against Communist rule, there was a small window of time and open border that allowed refugees to escape to the West. President Eisenhower established a commission and reported to Congress in January 1957 that he instituted a program for vetting and accepting these refugees, some of whom arrived by Thanksgiving 1956 in the United States. 35,000 Hungarian refugees were admitted by September 1957.[38]

1950 to 1960 Decade Immigration Numbers

According to Wikipedia, "From 1950 to 1960, the U.S. had 2,515,000 new immigrants with 477,000 arriving from Germany, 185,000 from Italy, 52,000 from the Netherlands, 203,000 from the UK, 46,000 from Japan, 300,000 from Mexico, and 377,000 from Canada."[39]

1965 Immigration and Nationality Act (Hart-Celler Act)

The Immigration and Nationality Act of 1965 changed the immigration patterns by eliminating the quota system. Replacing the quota system was job skills "giving particular preference to potential immigrants with relatives in the United States and with occupations deemed critical by the U.S. Department of Labor."[40]

Although the authors of the bill expected the chief beneficiaries would be those from Southern Europe with the small quotas as provided in the 1924 Act, by 1970, immigration greatly accelerated from countries such as Korea, China, India, the Philippines and Pakistan, along with African countries.[40]

1966 Cuban Adjustment Act

The Cuban Adjustment Act of 1966 gave permanent resident status to Cubans if they physically were present in the United States after January 1, 1959. The Castro led Communist revolution in Cuba in 1959 had driven the upper and middle classes into exile with most arriving by boat in Florida. By 1970, 409,000 immigrated to the United States.[41]

1986 Immigration Reform and Control Act (Simpson-Mazzoli Act)

The Immigration Reform and Control Act was passed in 1986 and was signed into law by President Reagan. The key provisions of the Act:

1. Required employers to attest to the immigration status of all employees.
2. Made it illegal to hire or recruit illegal immigrants "knowingly."
3. Legalized seasonal agricultural undocumented immigrants
4. Legalized undocumented immigrants who entered the U.S. prior to January 1, 1982 and resided there continuously with the penalty of a fine, payment of back taxes, admission of guilt, proof they were not guilty of any crimes, that they were in the U.S. before January 1, 1982, and they possessed at least a minimal knowledge about U.S. history, government and English language.[42]

"At the time, the Immigration and Naturalization Service estimated that about four million illegal immigrants would apply for legal status through the Act and roughly half would be eligible."[42]
In actuality, 3,000,000 were accepted.[43]

1996 Illegal Immigration Reform and Immigration Responsibility Act

This was comprehensive immigration reform designed to restructure and strengthen laws for both admissions and deportations of immigrants, especially for asylum seekers. Furthermore, it restructured immigration enforcement and attempted to limit and eliminate undocumented aliens from migrating to the U.S through closer federal and local jurisdiction coordination.

1. Asylum: The Act narrowed asylum criteria from the 1980 Refugee Act to attempt to prevent fraudulent filings by those migrating for economic or work-related reasons and imposing a filing deadline called "The One Year Bar."[44]
An exception window was provided for an asylum seeker to prove either there was a changed or extraordinary circumstance associated with the asylum seeker. It also precluded appeals to denied applications, added a higher processing fee, and gave enforcement officers, rather than judges the authority to determine expedited removal.[44]

2. Law Enforcement: The Act expanded the number of Border Patrol agents and allowed the Attorney General of the United States to obtain resources from other federal agencies to assist the Border Patrol as needed. While provisions were made to improve infrastructure and barriers along U.S. borders, whatever they were, they were ineffective. Penalties were stiffened for illegal entry and racketeering including alien smuggling and document fraud. More features included:

a.) Enhanced tracking systems on illegal aliens already present to detect specific employment   eligibility and visa stay violations.
b.) Creating counterfeit-resistant identification forms.
c.) Three to ten-year re-entry bars and future exclusion.

d.) Mandatory detention.

e.) Revocation status and removal for violent crimes.

f.) Redefinition of public health criteria and a tier system for access to public health benefits prioritized in order from top to bottom as citizen, legal immigrant, refugee, and illegal immigrant).

g.) Adding criteria and strengthening financial self-sufficiency guidelines of sponsors.

3. Coordination: Delegation of law enforcement to state and local law enforcement agencies was added through what are termed "287(g) Agreements.[44]

CHAPTER 3

UNDESIREABLE ILLEGAL ALIEN ISSUES

Illegal Aliens have no rights except to life. For murderers, rapists, sex traffickers, gangs, drug mules, and other heinous criminals, even the right to life is questionable. That is an objective statement. Someone has to throw out the trash.

We need a new committee in Congress on Unamerican Activities with the authority to punish and deport those who hold allegiances to other countries, who refuse to learn English, who are morally corrupt, who lack education, and who espouse the tenets of ignorant socialism and communism while trying to change American laws to those they hold onto in their old country of origin. Enforcement includes the U.S. Marshalls and Border Patrol. Courts are not needed.

In my research I discovered a website by Americans for Illegal Immigration (ALIPAC). I had already picked a few of the issues to highlight in this chapter, but the enumeration of the issues with illegal immigration is massive. Some of the major issues deal with the costs to federal and state government, criminal activities personal and impersonal against Americans, and medical concerns of individual transportation of diseases once conquered in the United States.

The issues are really overwhelming. What a great society we would have if we stopped illegal immigration in its tracks! I can only imagine what America could have been now. No wonder President Trump has the campaign slogan, "Make America Great Again." We have lost our way, given away our birthright, sold out our country to the nefarious, damaged our citizens irrevocably, and ruined out society with our policies. Here is the list for you to consider and do something about:

- [1] Anchor Babies: Birthright Citizenship Exploited
- Anti-American Attitudes
- Anti-Semitic Attitudes
- Attacks on Border Patrol and Law Enforcement Agents
- Attacks on Free Speech in America
- Animal Abuse Increases
- Census Numbers: Negative Impact on Congressional Representation
- Civil rights: Devalued by comparison to illegal actions
- Child Endangerment
- Child Molestation
- Closed and Overcrowded Hospitals and Emergency Rooms
- Cost of Translators
- Consulates issuing Matricular Cards (ID Mexico won't even accept)
- Day Laborers loitering and creating public hazards
- Depreciated Wages for Americans and Legal Immigrants
- Deterioration of Common American Culture
- Desecration of the American Flag: Foreign Flags used aggressively
- Disrespect for American Laws
- Document Fraud
- Drunk driving injuries and deaths: Hit and Runs
- Ethnic Cleansing and Race Riots
- Farm animals within city limits
- Food Poisoning
- Foreign Influence on US Politics

- Gangs, Graffiti, Drugs, Cartels, Smugglers, and Violence
- Gang Rape and unreported rapes
- High Birth Rates and Overpopulation
- Human Sex Slavery
- Identity Theft
- Increased Crime
- Increased Taxes for Americans
- Increased pressures on infrastructure (roads, traffic, water, sewer)
- Infectious Diseases
- Lost American Jobs
- Lost American Sovereignty
- Lost Self Governance of American citizens Vs. Globalism and Elitism
- Male Chauvinism: Gender inequality
- Not Speaking English, loss of common language, Press 1 for English
- Overcrowded Schools and Negative Impact on American Education
- Overcrowded single family homes
- Overcrowded Jails and Prisons
- Public Sanitation Loss: Trash and human waste in towns
- Racist Groups and Race Based Politics
- Remittances: Billions of dollars sent out of the US Economy
- Rule of Law: Fundamental principles of America sacrificed.
- Separatist Movements: Demands for autonomy
- Smear Campaigns and Lies: Dirty Politics
- Stolen American Taxpayer Resources: Tuition, Welfare, Licenses

- Taking limited seats in colleges at taxpayer expense via in-state tuition for illegals
- Taxpayer funds going to special interest groups (example) La Raza
- Terrorism Threats and Loss of national security
- Trash and Negative Impact on Environment at border
- Unfair to Legal Immigrants
- Unfair Business Competition for law abiding companies
- Unlicensed and Uninsured Motorists
- Untaxed Wages
- Voter Fraud

That is 54 counts against illegal aliens and the list is not complete. Take my treatment in Chapter 8 of eight more issues I had in mind when starting this book. In some sense they may be covered by the other 54, but I prepared the list in advance of the research and there is no direct match to the eight things that came to my mind immediately besides the major ones. That makes the new list 62 issues.

CHAPTER 4

ILLEGAL ALIEN COST TO AMERICA

Illegal immigration is the second greatest internal threat to our country regardless of the segment of the population; however, illegal immigration negatively affects those of us in the Gray Zone (50+) disproportionately. We all are direct or indirect victims whether it be illegal welfare payments, hospital cost increases to cover nonpaying illegals, education costs including adding classrooms and teachers, dangerous drug importation, sex trafficking of women and children, documented rape of innocent victims that involve our children and grandchildren, or murder of American citizens including couples and individuals. Then we get to subsidize them through the various welfare programs including illegal subsidies through Medicaid loopholes.

The greatest threat is "immigrants' brought to America from the Middle East. The third greatest threat is socialism.

In the 2018 midterm elections, Illegal Immigration was a hot button topic. This is illustrated in a Rasmussen Report national survey, "According to the latest Rasmussen Reports national survey, 72 percent of likely U.S. voters say that the issue of illegal immigration is important to their vote in the midterm elections this fall, with 42 percent saying it is "very important."[1] The question then is on which side are they?

Yes, I am still being objective! The far left asks how can I be, or how is that by your words? My answer is consider the logic first and how we are all affected second.

Logic alone dictates a powerful defense on American borders. You may call it horse sense or common sense, but it adds up to the same thing. For decades, even centuries we felt secure with Canada to the north, oceans on either side of the continental United States, and relative control of our southern border with Mexico. What has changed the most is the nature of the southern border. The problem has been recognized for decades and several administrations, but both parties let it fester.

The reason why it festered was businesses were reluctant to give up their cheap labor and migrant workers had become a normalized feature of picking crops in California's San Joaquin Valley among other things and places. The *bracero* program brought thousands of workers to the United States when labor was needed starting with World War II. That program did not envision invasion.

I have only to ask two questions:

1. Is America a country or a world province?
2. Are you IN FAVOR of a high crime rate caused by illegals, drugs continuing to flood our streets causing untold economic loss and citizen debilitation ending in early death, sex trafficking of women and children, exposure to third world diseases, wasting our resources on people who do not have the right to our free goods and services, the multibillion dollar cost of assistance programs, and further economic loss through remittances back to their home country, voter fraud, false Congressional representation, OR AGAINST?

Those are objective criteria for humanity and the preservation of any society. Now I hear the faint question, Don't you have compassion for them? My answer is another question, Don't you have compassion for Americans, for our elderly citizens, for our homeless, for our veterans, for our taxpayers, for the health and welfare of our own children?

Then I hear the strident voices that they just want to come to our country like our forefathers and mothers did.

That give me this feeling in the pit of my stomach that makes me angrily rise from where I am sitting and lambaste fools for equating those who come here to rape, rob, and ruin our society these days from those of our ancestors who came legally, who were processed properly, and who became law abiding citizens for the most part in our great melting pot. Some of the illegal immigrants could have made it here legally.

Only legally processed immigrants are acceptable. They are checked by visa issuing officers for their backgrounds with agency checks and must go through medical screening to be accepted. I know. I served as Visa issuing officer when the State Department Visa Issuing Officer in Vladivostok, Russia went on vacation. I was a diplomat with the US Department of Commerce and had the additional duty of Visa Issuing Officer for the US Department of State as agreed, approved, and studied at US Foreign Service Institute in Washington, DC.

The illegal immigrants and those who were scraped up from the Middle East who bring their own flags, refuse to assimilate, attempt to have their law replace American law, struggle to upend our great Republic, and aggressively seek to even vote, when they do not deserve to have that privilege, do not deserve the right looting our treasuries (federal and state), preying upon our citizens, as if we were subjects beholden to them, while living off the largesse of our welfare system.

If you do not live on the border of Mexico in one of four states: California, Texas, New Mexico, and Arizona you do not understand the threat to ranchers and their families on a daily basis. Although you may not live on the border, the threat to you is as real as being there facing hordes by yourself. You just fail to see and understand the problem.

Recently I have seen letters posted on social media from the wives of ranchers on the border that they have been intimated by groups of illegal immigrants, that they were stealing from the ranch, and that neighbors had been murdered!

I am not assigning blame to one political party or another, but to both American political parties. There are laws on the books such as fining a business for employing illegal aliens, but how many cases have your heard that were brought against them? I thought so. Hardly any unless a political figure was involved.

Pick a number with a lower end range from $3.3 Billion to 15.6 Billion[2] and then a high number of say the number used in 2017 by the Federation for American Immigration Reform (FAIR) of $155 Billion.[3] Cato Institute suggested the bottom range leaving out a host of taxes and other associated costs as well as trying to add the cost of more Border Patrol, when it should be reduced. In fact as analyst, Steven A. Camarota of FAIR, wrote in an article on May 1, 2017, "Even Cato Agrees: A Border Wall Can Pay for Itself."[4]

Estimates of the high cost of illegal immigration are like attempting to discover the number of demons that can dance on the head of a pin. In other words they are relevant only in the sense that there is an undisputed cost of some billions. If $15 Billion were put into building the wall, even Cato would have to admit in less than 5 years it would pay for itself. I believe the avalanche of articles detailing much higher costs.

Why did I suggest irrelevancy? Three reasons: 1.) None of them count the damages done by criminal activity. 2.) I refuse to believe there is a complete picture of the number of illegals in this country. 3.) Lost wages by American labor. They are irrelevant in that the greater arguments to cost are the damages done to Americans directly and indirectly through crime and incarceration.

When I lived in California. I was a Vice President for a company seeking to build apartments in Victorville. I visited other sites and the Project Managers and Construction Supervisors said they employed illegals to cut the costs of manpower on construction jobs. I observed numerous groups of them working on the projects I visited and they were pointed out to me.

I often was on a road connecting Interstate-5 with Interstate-15. At a juncture half way to Oceanside, I sometimes stopped for gas and a sandwich at McDonalds. Depending on the time of day there were upwards of 50 apparent illegal immigrants waiting to be picked up by someone for a day of work. I know they were illegal from having to talk to some looking for work and someone acting as a poor interpreter for them. I really hated to stop after a while, because they were becoming more aggressive, virtually blocking my car. They also made themselves scarce one day when a group of Californians appeared in pickup trucks with signs against illegal immigrants.

I mentioned the Cato Institute and FAIR. The Cato Institute is on the small end of the estimates and FAIR is on the large end. According to one article: "Cato Flubs Illegal Immigrant Numbers When Criticizing President Trump. This suggests that Cato underestimated the number of illegal immigrants by a significant amount even though they inappropriately claim 'we likely overestimate the number of illegal immigrants who are incarcerated." "Regardless of the estimates, the actual CATO numbers do not add up.'"[5]

Economic Cost

FAIR estimates the number of illegal immigrants at about 12.5 million[4] while the CATO Institute estimates a million less.[4] I have the gall and the right to suggest that either estimate is half the number. How do you quantify the hidden numbers in our country? The answer is you can only quantify the visible part. The visible part is somewhere in the billions of dollars cost to federal and state governments. Is that not enough to call a halt to the waste or resources and blocking out further erosion of our economy? I believe it is!

When I observe an evil that is becoming pervasive, my first tactic is to go to an extreme and ask the question, is that worth it? Take religion as an example. Would you approve of a cult that sacrificed women and children on a public altar and allow it to operate in the United States.

Unfortunately there seems to be a growing number of far-left people in our country who might accept such a cult these days and most of them are on the far-left wing of the Democratic Party. Now let me tell you I am thinking of the Aztecs and their religious cult. Where are you politically now?

Similarly I categorically state that even the loss of one dollar of taxpayer funds is too much and must be stopped at whatever the cost when coupled with the social ills that come with the problem.

Illegal Immigrant Welfare

I found a rather dated source of information on welfare use from 2011 by the Center for Immigration Studies. Although it is eight years old, it provides an excellent insight and one can multiply by whatever factor they want to for a 2019 figure.

Unsurprisingly, Census Bureau data collected by a nonpartisan Washington, DC group reveals most U.S. families headed by illegal immigrants use taxpayer-funded welfare programs on their American-born anchor babies at consistently higher rates than natives.[16]

"States in which immigrant household with children have the highest welfare costs are Arizona with 62%, Texas, California, and New York each with 61% and Pennsylvania with 59%.[7]

The study focused on eight major welfare programs that cost the government $517 billion the year they were examined. They include Supplemental Security Income (SSI) for the disabled, Temporary Assistance to Needy Families (TANF), a nutritional program known as Women, Infants and Children (WIC), food stamps, free/reduced school lunch, public housing and health insurance for the poor (Medicaid).

Food assistance and Medicaid are the programs most commonly used by illegal immigrants, mainly on behalf of their American-born children who get automatic citizenship. Legal immigrant households take advantage of every available welfare program, according to the study, which attributes it to low education level and resulting low income.[8]

The highest rates of welfare recipients come from the Dominican Republic (82%), Mexico and Guatemala (75% each) and Ecuador (70%). Welfare use is high for both new arrivals and established residents.[8]

Medicaid

Although illegal immigrants are disqualified from receiving Medicaid benefits, they do cost American taxpayers $18.5 Billion annually. Chris Conover writing in Forbes stated, "All told, Americans cross-subsidize health care for unauthorized immigrants to the tune of $18.5 billion a year. Of this total, federal taxpayers provided $11.2 billion in subsidized care to unauthorized immigrants in 2016."[9]

"That is one of the reasons the Social Security system is increasingly becoming insolvent as the years go along. This constitutes stealing from those of us who paid into the system and are paying now."[10]

As always once a fund has been "pierced," to use a legal term, the losses continue to grow. "The Center for Immigration Studies (CIS) found that the percentage of new immigrants on Medicaid grew from six percent in 2007 to 17 percent in 2017 – an increase of 11 percentage points. The percentage of Americans on Medicaid also slightly increased during the same time period, by nine percent."[11] Furthermore,

"The average immigrant household consumes 33 percent more cash welfare, 57 percent more food assistance, and 44 percent more Medicaid dollars than the average native household,"[12]

Loopholes

1. <u>Medicaid and Medicare Subsidies</u>. If this is illegal, how does this get siphoned and why has it not been cut off? The regulations are strict even in the Affordable Care Act, but loopholes exist, such as an indirect receipt of $2.8 Billion states Medicaid programs and "through federal taxes totaling at least $4.6 Billion."[13]

According to a report from the Henry J. Kaiser Family Foundation, the states of New York, Washington, Illinois, Massachusetts, California plus the District of Columbia "all provide state-only Medicaid benefits to illegal immigrants."[14]

2. <u>Community Health Centers.</u> Federal taxes indirectly fund these centers.

3. <u>Hospitals and Other Health Centers</u>. Many of these facilities are tax exempt.

> "Federal law requires that state Medicaid programs make Disproportionate Share Hospital (DSH) payments to qualifying hospitals that care for a large number of Medicaid and uninsured individuals. Because these hospitals are not restricted from using uncompensated care funds on illegal immigrants, the DSH Medicare and Medicaid payments they receive indirectly fund aggregate uncompensated care losses from illegal immigrants."[15]

4. <u>**Employer Tax Exclusions**</u>. This is not only a loophole, but an unwarranted exclusion rewarding employers for doing the wrong thing.

Below are the State-by-State Costs of Illegal Alien Immigrants excluding Federal Government costs as reported way back in 2011.

Table 3-1

https://www.judicialwatch.org/blog/2011/04/most-illegal-immigrant-families-collect-welfare/

Remittances

Remittances to foreign countries is a major loss of revenue that has been equated to a tax on America by other countries.[16] There is a lot of vitriol on the subject of remittances from one side believing it helps relatives in poor countries, helps the poor countries themselves and is worth the chance of them falling into the hands of drug cartels. The other side contends that is money that should be kept in the

United States because it counts against our currency strength, that there are better ways to help poor countries with aid programs already in place and that it lines pockets in the long run of either Carlos Slim (the richest Mexican we know) or drug cartels.[17]

The top country receiving American dollars on an annual basis is Mexico followed by other Central American Countries. The problem is a lot of this money is also going to Drug Cartels. In 2015, Mexico received $24.4 Billion alone representing approximately 2% of the nations' economy. Remittances in 2015 surpassed oil exports as a revenue earner for Mexico for the first time in country history.[17]

I like the metaphor of one article titled, "Finding the Right Ballpark."[17] That is because no one has the "right bat" to play the game, if I may be permitted to extend the metaphor. "Reasonable assumptions" have to be made from a "reasonable set of data." If you have been reading this book and understand the way I think, the enormity of the situation is already attested to by the fact that the "ballgames" are played at high stakes. Quibbling over methodology is better left to the analysts who present their assumptions and data and then defend it against all comers.

As the various articles admit, there is no precise data on how much is remitted annually. We know from all of them that it is in the billions. Like I say, that is all I need to know for the figure that is finally used as long as the method of deriving the data is presented. You are going to ask though, why we do not know.

1. The number of illegal aliens residing in the U.S. is less than precise by millions.
2. "The term remittance itself is ambiguous: should we include money stuffed in a birthday card?"[17]
3. We cannot track every dollar.
4. We are uncertain of who are the actual recipients. Do

they wind up with the intended relatives, or do they get "taxed" on the way by gangs?

5. Are the remittances from first-generation legal immigrants or illegal aliens?

Finding the closest correct methodology involves critical thinking and then make assumptions like percent of remittance likely to be from each source. Dividing up the money into percentages by groups with assumptions about sending equal or unequal amounts of earnings is tricky, but the only way to arrive at a "reasonable" estimate.

According to a report by Pew Research regarding 2016 remittances to other countries, the outflow from the United States was $138.2 Billion.[18] Pew Research further showed the significance of the payments to some countries using El Salvador as one of the countries with the greatest dependency on the United State remittances. I just mentioned that for Mexico in 2015, it was estimated at around 2% of GDP, but for El Salvador, remittances from abroad were 17.1% of the GDP in 2016, of which 90% came from the estimated 200,000 living in the United States.[19]

In making the case from a conservative standpoint, Spencer P. Morrison began his methodology with the closest accepted facts that there are 40 million first-generation immigrants and "(at least)" 11.1 million illegal aliens for a total just over 51 million.[20]

As I have suggested the illegal immigrant figure is far below the actual numbers that I believe are here. The analysis by Morrison presented a "recent study from Yale University" that there are at least 22.8 million illegals residing in the United States.[21] For the methodology Morrison then went with the 11.1 million as being the one most acceptable to all parties.

Like I said, it should not matter to us, since the problem is like an elephant—it is enormous and right in front of us. We can see it unless we are blind. Morrison came up will $30 billion likely remitted by illegals and likened it to the entire annual Gross Domestic Product of Vermont.[22] Of course he slams the liberal Cato Institute for "routinely arguing in favor of open borders and for their repeated failure to grasp the significant of the losses to our own economy, in which Economists of every stripe tell us the turnover of money in our own economy has a multiplier effect and that investment is lost. That loss then actually corresponds to $300 million to $600 million lost to the United States given a multiplier effect either of 10:1 or up to 20:1.[23]

I added the multiplier effect so you could understand the significance of the loss. I minored in Economics, by the way. Remember this is without using the Yale figures for estimated number of illegals hidden away in our interior.

For the record, according to a World Bank Report, migrants both legal and illegal forwarded $53.4 Million in remittances to Mexico and Central America in 2018.[123] Remittances to Mexico alone reached $33.7 Billion in 2018, which was up by 21% over the 2016 figure of $27.8 Billion, and $19.7 Billion to the rest of central America, which also was up from $15.8 Billion in 2016.[24]

According to Breitbart, GOP legislators suggested a tax be placed on sending remittances. He adds, "The money sent back from the United States to Central America includes many migrants' payments to the cartels who traffic them into the U.S. economy. The trafficking debts can start at $5,000 per head."[25]

There are more questions to be asked about remittances, although the size of the total added to costs associated with taking care of illegal aliens brings the total to at least $200 Billion annually. Point made! Enough said!

CHAPTER 5

MEDICAL COSTS AND STRAIN OF ILLEGAL ALIENS

Diseases

Feel good stories are about Doctors without Borders going to Central America and treating tropical diseases and diseases that the United States once conquered like bubonic plague, chicken pox, measles, mumps, tuberculosis, scarlet fever and whooping cough. Suddenly these diseases are reappearing in the last few years and the cause is illegal immigrants. Legal immigrants get checked and get vaccinated before coming to the U.S.

I am incredulous at the numbers of illegals who bring long past diseases conquered in the United States with them and begin infections nationwide. I am also incredulous that public health agencies like the CDC have not been tasked to come up with comprehensive statistics and tables concerning these diseases and from where they are coming. I had to rely on various sources for some of the data.

The first thing I learned is that states like California are warned by the political establishment there to forego reporting on the subject. The second thing I learned is that horrific diseases are brought here by their human vectors at an alarming rate and infecting our country when we had public health control in the past. They are truly a chaotic caravan of a vast array of diseases. The third thing I learned is that organizations that are pro-immigration have produced fake news promulgating the fact that these diseases are good for us to improve our health (somehow), that there are a few, and that we should just deal with it.

Wrong! Diseases are the bane and fear of the elderly. Those of us in the Gray Zone once felt comfortable that a flu shot annually and pneumonia shot would solve any disease transmission problem. We have lost our confidence now in public health and in politicians that struggle against the real facts of the situation.

Infections on an unprecedented magnitude are coming to America with illegal immigrants. We contact them in retail stores, businesses, construction sites, and restaurants. Our school age grandchildren and police forces come in contact on a daily basis, let along the poor Border Patrol agents and other law enforcement authorities.

First, I will detail a report in the Dark Side of Illegal Immigration describing various diseases.[1] Don't anyone disparage this report, since there are a variety of public sources that can be found on a disease by disease case. The information is dated though, so guess how much has transpired in a decade. Then I will incorporate material from 2015-2016 on duplicate diseases with square parentheticals [ ]. Here are the major diseases in the earlier report:

Dark Side Listings

1. Malaria. Malaria was eradicated from the USA in the 1940's. Now there have been recent outbreaks in Southern California, New Jersey, New York City and Houston. Besides that "Malaria tainted blood has been discovered in the blood supply."[1]

2. Dengue Fever. Previously unknown in the U.S. "Dengue outbreaks have now occurred in the United States.

3. Leprosy (Now called Hansen's Disease). "In the 40 years prior to 2002, there were only 900 total cases…in the US. In the following three years there have been 9,000 cases and most were illegal aliens." The Breitbart article referred to an article by Dr. William Levis, Head of New York Hansen's Disease, title "Leprosy in America: New Cause for Concern," who said New York is endemic now, and nobody's noticed. Likewise Dr, Terry Williams in Houston, who runs a clinic serving leprosy patients from across South Texas said the bulk of cases were immigrants.

4. Tuberculosis. "In an article in the Journal of the American Medical Association, Dr. Reuben Granich, a lead investigator for the CDC commented on MDR-TB: 'Evidence of it has surfaced in 38 of 61 California health jurisdictions, and it could 'threaten the efficacy of TB control efforts,' Granich said. The infected were said to be four times as likely to die from the disease and twice as likely to transmit the disease to others ... Reluctant to label the infected as 'illegal' or even 'undocumented' aliens, the report notes that of the 407 known cases of MDR-TB, 84% were 'foreign-born' patients, mainly from Mexico and the Philippines who'd been in the U.S. less than five years.'"[11]

[TB active/communicable cases tripled percentage wise for foreign born residents in the U.S. from 22 percent in 1986 to 66% of the active cases of 9.563. There were only 3,200 cases in 2015 of Native Americans and 6,300 reported of foreign-born cases mostly Mexico and the Philippines. Furthermore the spread is all over the U.S. As reported in Breitbart News: "In the past five years, 21 in Louisiana, 10 in Colorado, 4 in Indiana, 11 in Florida, and 9 in one county of Kentucky. Latent cases were 26% in Indiana, 22% in Minnesota, 15% in Texas, and 12% in California."][2]

5. Chagas Disease (Trypanosomiasis). This disease is endemic to South and Central America through a bug that bites people. "It was unknown in the United States until fairly recently. It is now (2006) estimated that between 100,000 and 500,000 people in the US have Chagas Disease. Who is infect? Mostly illegal aliens."[1]

6. HIV. "The number of illegal Mexican and Central American immigrants with HIV or AIDS is unknown, mostly because researchers rarely ask about immigration status. However, it is known that the rate of HIV infection among Latino women in California is about twice the rate of white women. At one free California health clinic, all of the women have HIV or AIDS. Most are Mexican or Central American 'immigrants.'"[1]

CDC and Breitbart Report[2]

1. Measles: The CDC reported a record number of cases for the past 40 years when in 2014 the U.S. had 667 cases from 27 states reported to the CDC National Center for Immunization and Respiratory Diseases (NCIRD). It was documented measles had been eliminated in the U.S. by 2000. In 2019 we can watch on the daily news discussions of the need and/or resistance to getting vaccinations. Cases over the past four years were documented in Arizona, California, Georgia, Hawaii, Illinois, Massachusetts, Minnesota and DC. Then in 2016 one case was in a mosque in Memphis.

2. Pertusis (Whooping Cough): In 1926, over 200,000 had whooping cough in the US. In 1976, it had been reduced through vaccinations to 1,010. It crept back with gradual increases in illegal immigrants to over 4,000 in 1986. **In 2014 reported cases grew from 1,010 in 1976, to 32,971 cases. There is no doubt the cause is immigrants either those hoisted from the Middle East or those illegals flowing across our Southern Border.**

3. Other: Add mumps to the mix along with a host of other diseases including intestinal parasites, scabies, diphtheria, flesh eating bacteria and parasites, and Ebola (mainly from the African Continent).

Judicial Watch Medical Report, 2019

"Weeks after mainstream media outlets reported that illegal immigrants don't bring disease into the United States, the Border Patrol reveals that it is getting slammed daily with dozens of illegal immigrants carrying "serious illnesses." This includes tuberculosis, influenza and pneumonia. In fact, a Guatemalan migrant who died in U.S. custody on Christmas Eve had Influenza B, a virus that causes respiratory infections. Federal agents are referring 50 illegal immigrants a day for urgent medical care, according to figures obtained by Washington D.C.'s conservative newspaper. Authorities say "it's unlike anything they've ever seen before." Many of the migrants have tuberculosis, parasites or the flue, the feds confirm. There are also lots of pregnant women about to give birth. The article quotes Customs and Border Protection (CBP) Commissioner Kevin McAleenan saying that most of the illegal immigrants were sick when they arrived at the U.S. border. "Many were ill before they departed their homes," McAleenan said. "We're talking about cases of pneumonia, tuberculosis, parasites. These are not things that developed urgently in a matter of days."[12]

"…the Coast Guard has been deployed to help, sending medical teams to Border Patrol sectors getting bombarded with sick migrants. They include Yuma and Tucson, Arizona as well as the Rio Grande Valley."[12]

"The biased coverage marked a great example of the mainstream media distorting information to promote a liberal agenda."[12]

"Judicial Watch interviewed medical experts who

confirmed illegal immigrants do pose a serious public health threat by bringing dangerous diseases into the U.S.. This includes tuberculosis, dengue and Chikungunya. After returning from covering the Central American caravan along the Guatemala-Honduras border, Judicial Watch spoke with a prominent physician in a border state who **warned** that the migrants will undoubtedly bring infectious diseases into the U.S. Among them are extremely drug resistant strands of tuberculosis and mosquito-borne diseases: dengue and chikungunya that are widespread in the region."[13]

"Years ago, when Barack Obama let tens of thousands of illegal immigrant minors into the country, health experts warned about the serious hazards to the American public. Most of the Unaccompanied Alien Children (UAC) came from Central America...and they crossed into the U.S. through Mexico... Swine flu, dengue fever and Ebola were among the diseases that the hordes of UACs brought with them, according to lawmakers and medical experts interviewed by Judicial Watch during the influx...A U.S. Congressman, who is also a medical doctor, told Judicial Watch about the danger to the American public as well as the Border Patrol agents forced to care for the UACs. The former lawmaker, Phil Gingrey, referred to it as a "severe and dangerous" crisis because the Central American youths were importing infectious diseases considered to be largely eradicated in this country. Many migrants lack basic vaccinations such as those to prevent chicken pox or measles, leaving America's young children and the elderly particularly susceptible, Gingrey pointed out then. To handle the escalating health crisis the CDC activated an Emergency Operations Center (EOC) that largely operated in secrecy."[3]

CHAPTER 6

ILLEGAL ALIENS AND POLITICS

2020 Decennial Census Controversy over the Question of U.S. Citizenship

The U.S. Census is important to states for three reasons: 1) Number of Representatives in Congress, 2.) Distribution of federal funds, and 3.) Electoral College Votes. All of these issues are incendiary and worth all sides fighting over, not just for 2020, but going forward politically.

Take distribution of federal funds. $900 billion is distributed from the federal government annually to the states and apportioned according to the census data. The money is used for schools, hospitals, roads, health care and a lot more.

The question of adding in some form the question of U.S. Citizenship for each family and each member of a household generated a suit by California, joined by other states with the desire to delete the question of U.S. Citizenship. California's main argument was people would not submit their forms, or would not include all the persons in the household. That was a smoke screen.

California's real concern was prompted by a certainty that they would lose overall population count for the purpose of adding Representatives to the House of Representatives in Congress and they would lose a portion of grants and federal funding for programs based on population.

What are the facts concerning the 2020 census citizenship question? Some claim it has always been part of the census in some form, while others point out the lapses in the short census form.

The precedent for asking the citizenship question goes way back in U.S. history to the census of 1820. Some form of this question was on the 1830 and 1870 census. Certainly it was asked of the entire U.S. population from the 1890 to 1950 census.[1]

In 1960, the question was not asked. According to a Pew Research Report, "Since then, the citizenship question has been asked of only a sample of households, either on the census long form of the American Community Survey, which replaced the form in 2010."[2] The 1960 census did have place of birth.

U.S. Marshals were the first census takers. Later surveys were sent by mail to most American households. That was supplemented by census takers who were tasked during the year to contact those households that did not promptly respond. The last full citizenship survey in 1950 asked "where each person was born and in a follow-up question asked, 'If foreign born – Is he naturalized?'"[3]

The 1970 census introduced the short form questionnaire without the citizenship question, but it was still on the long form. The short form went to the large majority of households and the long form to a much smaller sample of 1 in 6 households with the question intact.[4] The 2000 long form did ask the question specifically, "Is this person a CITIZEN of the United States?"[5]

Starting in 1996, The U.S. Census Bureau began a yearly survey of 3.5 million U.S. households to collect information previously contained only in the long form of decennial census. This was titled the American Community Survey (ACS). 1996 was the demonstration project, that was expanded in 1997, and by 2005 was fully operational. This became the basis for the 2010 census, when the question of citizenship was omitted from both the long and short forms. One has to question the effectiveness of such a small sample of the population.[6]

The questions are about ancestry, educational attainment, income, language proficiency, migration, employment, disabilities and housing characteristics. The responses are important for government purposes such as funding and to the private sector for marketing requirements.

By law, the individual responses are kept confidential. That includes the FBI and other government entities. The U.S. Department of Commerce contains the Census Bureau and manages both the ACS and the decennial census.

While California raised the question about failure to participate, The U.S. Department of Commerce Secretary, Wilbur Ross, dismissed it in a memo as follows:

"The Department of Commerce is not able to determine definitively how inclusion of a citizenship question on the decennial census will impact responsiveness. However, even if there is some impact on responses, the value of more complete and accurate data derived from surveying the entire population outweighs such concerns. Completing and returning decennial census questionnaires is required by Federal law, those responses are protected by law, and inclusion of a citizenship question on the 2020 decennial census will provide more complete information for those who respond."[7]

Ross stated the 2020 Census Form would use the same wording as in the ACS. The ACS asks respondents to check one of five categories to describe their citizenship status. Three of those categories apply to U.S. citizens at birth: 1.) Born in the U.S. 2.) Born in a U.S. Territory. 3.) Born abroad to at least one U.S. citizen parent. The fourth category is those who are naturalized U.S. Citizens are further asked for their year of naturalization. The fifth category is checking the box "Not a

U.S. Citizen." There is no question on the ACS whether noncitizens are in the U.S. legally or illegally.[8]

Secretary Ross pointed out the citizenship question would be last on the form to minimize nonparticipation response rates. He the ordered the Census Bureau to use other federal and state government records to fill in missing responses.

In point of fact the Census Bureau already fills in missing date using the statistical technique of 'Imputation," from neighboring householder information. "In the 2010 census, imputation added more than a million people to the household population," filling in age, sex and race data.[9]

The Census Bureau is studying how to complete 2020 census forms using government records from Social Security, Internal Revenue Service and similar records. Besides that the census will be bounced off individual government records in order to establish and accurate ratio of citizen to non-citizen response for the purposes of imputation.[10]

2019 Temporary Supreme Court Block on Adding the Citizenship Question

On June 27, 2019, the U.S. Supreme Court issued a ruling 5-4 as a temporary measure to deleted the citizenship question from the U.S. 2020 Census Form. This started a firestorm between the Trump Administration, the states and those of the population for and against illegal aliens.

California took the lead in the suit. The reason it is critical to California is 28% of household residents there have an illegal alien living with them. The number is much higher in the Los Angeles area and would affect population representation for the House of Representatives in the U.S. Congress. The change also would affect federal funding for everything from schools to transportation.[11]

Soon after the Supreme Court heard the case brought by California and a number of other states and jurisdictions, the bitter battle continued for the purpose of placing the citizenship question on the national census form in 2020. Trump tweeted: "Can anyone really believe that as a great Country, we are not able (to) ask whether or not someone is a Citizen. Only in America!"[12]

Chief Justice John Roberts in delivering the majority opinion (5-4) made it clear that the Trump Administration needed a better set of explanations from them, suggesting a disconnect between the decision and the explanation. In his words, "If judicial review is to be more than an empty ritual, it must demand something better than the explanation offered for the action taken in this case."[13]

Challengers to the administrative ruling maintained that Secretary Ross was motivated only for political reasons. Ros countered with the need for citizenship information for purposes of enforcing the Voting Right Act.[14] Apparently that perfectly good answer was insufficient to satisfy the court.

This political hot potato has yet to make it to the frying pan.

Sovereignty

Sovereignty is the right to govern a territorial area and populace within those borders without any interference whatsoever from outside sources or bodies. That is my slightly reworked definition from dictionary sources. Sovereignty is the keystone in the arch for a national government to even exist.

I used to smile a little at graphics that had Native Americans saying they had open border and look what happened to them. I no longer even smile, since there is a new strain of criminal element in our country that does not want borders, border watchers, or border passage so they are free to commit crime, deal drugs, and engage in unfettered sex trafficking.

The Gray Zone citizens not only want borders, but needs them to begin feeling safer once again. Illegal immigrants are like the boogeyman in the room of a children who fears monsters. In this case some really are monsters. There is no choice other than to build walls, fences, obstacles, or anything else we can build to secure our people, not just in the Gray Zone, but our future citizens.

Illegals and "Rights"

Let us be very clear up front. Illegals have no rights, not to life, liberty, or the pursuit of happiness. There are judges and juries that have been convened in trials against ranchers in Arizona and other states in which illegals have sued ranchers for intimidation, capture, and causing fear. Those judges should have dismissed the suit outright.

Legal rights are accorded guests in the United States like tourists, green card holders, and others with visas of various kinds, but do these judges not understand basic legal principles? First, they have no "standing." They are illegally here for goodness sakes! By the way that is the strongest curse words I ever use.

Voter Fraud

The laughable part of the investigation into voter fraud is that the biggest fraud is now perpetrated by illegal aliens in the most recent elections of 2016 and 2018, not the Russians. Russians and Chinese, whether state actors, businesses, or simply with foreign individuals wanting to play games apparently were involved in influence peddling or election manipulation on some level, but it pales in relation to that perpetrated by illegal aliens and those parties and party position seekers who encourage them to vote.

That is voter fraud, aiding and abetting voter fraud, and anyone caught doing it must be punished. The Gray Zone demands it in order to restore public confidence to our electoral process.

If you believe some of the liberal fact checking organizations, then you are deluded. The process is easy to state one has the right to vote as a citizen. It is a box checked on driver license forms both when acquiring one and when renewing one. The following story from the Washington Times (2017) shows both the ease of acceptance and the difficulty of discovery. It also shows the penalty is permanent removal and deportation from the United States.

According to the United States 7th Circuit Court of Appeals in Illinois, "Non-citizens who register to vote are breaking federal laws and can be deported."[15]

"Margarita Del Pilar Fitzpatrick had registered to vote in Illinois, and had even cast ballots That was enough to trigger an American law that allows the government to kick out non-citizens who vote illegally...Ms. Fitzpatrick had registered to vote when she went to get a driver's license. Under the federal motor-voter law, she was given the option to check a box signaling she was a citizen and wanted to vote. "

"She said she asked the employee if she should check it, and the employee said, "it's up to you." In court, Ms. Fitzpatrick tried to raise that as a defense, with her lawyers saying it was equivalent to entrapment because a state official had told her to sign up. But the three-judge panel rejected that argument, saying the employee wasn't encouraging her, only telling her it was her choice."[16]

Ms. Fitzpatrick not only understood English in the case, but worked as a translator. The case only came to light, because she raised a flag on her 2007 application for citizenship, reporting that she had in fact previously registered to vote and voted despite laws against it.[17]

As I said, fact checkers dispute claims of voter fraud citing no evidence, but this case demonstrates the tiny tip of the problem in determining fraudulent voting and the extent of it unless someone's record is flagged and then the information is checked.

CHAPTER 7

CRIME AND ILLEGAL ALIENS

If even one crime is committed by an illegal alien, that is too much. It could have/should have been prevented. Any reasonable person would conclude that the billions of dollars lost and the threat manifested in crime in the United States because of illegal entrants is worth putting up a gargantuan well-protected wall.

Apparently we have people in Congress that either do not possess the good sense we, the logical and rational people of this country are given, or are profiting personally in some way. My own speculation is some must be accommodating drug dealers and receiving behind the back payments in return, using illegals for their own cheap labor supply in homes as domestics or businesses as laborers, or receiving political contributions. They return the favor by assisting them in the legislative process by helping to maintain a porous border.

There is an excellent study on all prisoners who entered the State of Arizona prison system from January 1985, through the end of June 2017, that separates non-U.S. citizens by whether or not they are illegal immigrants, or legal residents. Recognize in dealing with illegal immigrants, we are dealing only with the tip of the iceberg that can be seen, quantified and assessed. The numbers of crimes and the types of violent crimes they have committed are staggering.

From the report abstract, "Undocumented immigrants are at least 142% more likely to be convicted of a crime than other Arizonans. They also tend to commit more serious crimes and serve 10.5% longer sentences, more likely to be classified as dangerous, and 45% more likely to be gang members than U.S. citizens. Yet, there are several reasons that these numbers are likely to underestimate the share of crime committed by undocumented immigrants. There are dramatic differences in the criminal histories of convicts who are U.S. citizens and undocumented immigrants.....While undocumented immigrants from 15 to 35 years of age make up slightly over 2 percent of the Arizona population, they make up almost 8% of the prison population. Even after adjusting for the fact that young people commit crime at higher rates, young undocumented immigrants commit crime at twice the rate of young U.S. citizens. These undocumented immigrants also tend to commit more serious crimes."[1]

Chilling numbers are reflected here that the Gray Zone finds avoidable, reprehensible, and dereliction of the duty of our government to protect us, not to mention the personal cost, personal loss of our citizens, and fear that accompanies it. The study went on to make a scary extrapolation, "If undocumented immigrants committed crime nationally as they do in Arizona, in 2016 they would have been responsible for over 1,000 more murders, 5,200 rapes, 8,900 robberies, 25,300 aggravated assaults, and 26,900 burglaries.[2]

Do you need more evidence of the wholesale infliction of pain and suffering that unconscionably goes on under our very noses? Then I refer you to an earlier study by the Government Accountability Office (GAO) that was tasked to arrive at some numbers of illegal crimes in this country by type of offense committed. The figures given in the table show the numbers of illegal alien crimes for the period 2005 to 2010.[3]

The conclusion of the first study is: "Illegals and noncitizens make up 3% and 8% of the population respectively, but commit at least 22% to 37% of the murders. Illegals likely commit **murder** at around 10 times the rate of all

US inhabitants.....Around 6,000 people are killed by illegal aliens, almost all of whom are Latinos, every single year! "[4]

Table 6-1

Alien Criminal Offenses by Category
(2005-10)[5] and (2011-2016)[6]

Arrest Offense	Federal# 2005-10	Federal# 2011-2016	State# 2011-2016
Immigration	529,859	874,400	1,226,000
Drugs	504,043	336,600	761,200
Traffic	404,788	204,400	852,000
Assault	213,047	108,400	397,000
Larceny/Theft	125,322	70,300	276,700
Fraud, forgery, and counterfeiting	120,810	62,300	200,100
Obstruction of Justice	252,899	141,300	665,000
Burglary	115,045	44,900	175,000
Weapons violations	94,492	44,500	124,700
Motor Vehicle Theft	81,710	19,500	90,800
Sex Offenses	69,929	13,500	120,300
Disorderly Conduct	52,384	12,300	90,800
Stolen Property	49,126	14,300	75,500
Property Damage	42,609	17,500	x
Robbery	42,609	13,500	54,700
Homicide	25,064	6,000	x
Kidnappings	x	5,000	x
Arson	2,005	400	x
Terrorism	x	400	x
Other	151,138	74,200	257,000
Total	**2,891,668**	**2,016,400**	**5,402,900**

Notice the total of illegal immigrants incarcerated for both federal and state is **7,419,300!** The GAO report in 2018 noted 208,800 criminal aliens were in state and federal prisons at an annual cost to taxpayers of $1.42 Billion down a little from the $1.56 Billion from the previous report.[7]

The numbers are illustrative and anecdotal. I use them simply to provide the scope of the enormity of the problem. I have seen challenges and counterchallenges to the statistical methods used by everybody with claims and counterclaims and I frankly do not care. What do people not get about an enormous problem? Logic and common sense every American citizen.

Illegal Employment Practices of American Companies

American companies are forbidden to hire illegal immigrants, yet they do. When they are caught the fines can be stringent. I will present just on case brought by The United States Attorney's Office for the Eastern District of Tennessee.

"On September 12, 2018, James Brantley, 61, of Bean Station, Tennessee, pleaded guilty before the Honorable J. Ronnie Greer, U.S. District Judge, to tax fraud, wire fraud, and employment of unauthorized illegal aliens. Brantley is the owner of Southeastern Provision, LLC (Southeastern Provision), a slaughterhouse and meatpacking plant located in Bean Station, Tennessee.

Brantley faces up to five years in prison, a $250,000 fine, and three years of supervised release for the tax counts. He faces a maximum of 20 years in prison, a $250,000 fine, and three years of supervised release on the wire fraud charge. Finally, he faces up to six months in prison and a fine of not more than $3,000 per unauthorized alien on the employment of unauthorized alien charge. Brantley also agreed to pay restitution to the United States government in the total amount of $1,423,588 on or before the date of his sentencing. Sentencing has been set for 1:30 p.m., February 4,

2019, in U.S. District Court.....According to the plea agreement, beginning in 1988 and continuing through April 2018, Brantley knowingly hired, or caused others employed by him to hire, unauthorized aliens to work as employees at Southeastern Provision. The unauthorized aliens were knowingly hired to reduce Brantley and Southeastern Provision's FICA tax obligations, unemployment insurance premiums, unemployment tax obligations, and workers' compensation insurance premiums."[8]

The federal search warrant that was executed in April 2018, stated *"agents discovered at least 104 unauthorized aliens employed there. Evidence showed that Brantley had previously reported to the Internal Revenue Service (IRS) that he had only 44 wage-earning employees. Further investigation revealed that he paid the unauthorized aliens in cash at a rate of $8-$10 per hour. The employees were also often asked to work overtime at their standard rate of pay, rather than the 'time and a half' required by the Fair Labor Standards Act for overtime work."*[9]

I could provide a comprehensive litany of lessons about getting caught using illegal immigrants, however, I believe one story is sufficient for this book. If I added more, I would finally write my doctoral dissertation. The story though in the case described covers so many angles: why businesses hire illegals, why they pay "under the table and simultaneously cook their own books just like the illegal still owners used to do" (which accounts for the IRS working with ICE on the raid). I contend the fine of only $3,000 per illegal immigrant by itself would have really been worth it to the business, which is why more charges were levied including wire fraud. The raid included the IRS, ICE and Tennessee Highway Patrol.

You will find numerous studies, papers and articles by pro-immigration organizations such as those filing papers in this case defending not only the illegal immigrants, but filing suit against those that conducted the raid! *"The suit was filed in federal court in Knoxville by the National Immigration Law Center, the Southern Poverty Law Center, and the law firm of Sherrard,*

Roe, Voigt and Harbison….."[10] Thus there were two public advocacy groups and a law firm specializing in assisting illegal aliens in illegal immigrant cases.

I find it difficult to believe that anything could be filed again given the fact illegals have no standing in State or Federal Courts, but have been granted "illegal" access. Whatever happened to the legal determination of "standing?" That tells you when a legal system has gone corrupt is when those without standing still flood the courts.

Give the removal authority only to the federal U.S. Marshal Service. The service is the oldest federal law enforcement service with roots in 1789, when George Washington established it. Keep the U.S. Courts only for U.S. persons and cases. I know this will throw a lot of immigration attorneys out on the street, but surely they can find some other low-level legal issues to replace them.

Border States and Alien Crime

Border ranchers and landowners are suffering from an unprecedented heavy crime wave. The heavy increase began in the 1980's and has continued to accelerate in 2019. I read letters written by the wives of border ranchers on social media that tear the heart out. They report being under siege in their ranch house by gangs of illegal aliens all the way from Mexico to Honduras invading their property and threatening them with demands for food and even killing their husbands.

Even one crime is too much, but 24,746 filed in 2013 near the Mexican Border is a story that will not go away. Hope shameful and disgusting is Congress during the first four years of the Trump Administration to refuse all the help and assistance in preventing border crime with such a powerful visibility and societal repercussions.

Congress, especially the Democratic controlled House of Representatives (2019-2020) is to blame. President Trump has done the best he can to obtain funds to build the wall along the entire Southern border as it should have been done in the 1800s.

A 2014 report from the Department of Justice that I read via Judicial Watch, found the following information on crime from state in districts neighboring the Mexican border: **"Almost 50 percent of federal crimes were committed near the Mexican border."[11]**

"Of the 61,529 criminal cases initiated by federal prosecutors last fiscal year, more than 40% — or 24,746 — were filed in court districts neighboring the Mexican border. This includes Arizona, New Mexico, Southern California, Western Texas and Southern Texas. The two Texas districts each had more than double the convictions of all four federal court districts in the state of New York combined, according to the DOJ report. The Western Texas District had the nation's heaviest crime flow, with 6,341 cases filed by the feds. In Southern Texas 6,130 cases were filed, 4,848 in Southern California, 3,889 in New Mexico and 3,538 in Arizona. In fact, 38.6% of all federal cases (23,744) filed last year involved immigration, the DOJ report confirms. Nearly 22% (13,383) were drug related, 19.7% (12,123) were violent crimes and 10.2% (6,300) involved white-collar offenses that include a full range of frauds committed by business and government professionals. "[11]

Now try to answer to American citizens suffering from the illegal alien invasion on a daily basis that there is no need for a border wall. Notice the aiding and abetting of frauds by business professionals and government personnel.

Letters from Wives of Ranches on the Mexican Border

I personally am a member of two Texas oriented Facebook groups: 1.) Texas Fun and Facts, and 2.) This is Texas. Often there are postings I read from wives of ranchers who live on the Texas side of the border with Mexico. All of them relate the dangers from illegal aliens on their property who terrorize the wives, steal anything not nailed down, appear at the gates to the ranch house, cut or break down pasture fences and ram into gates. Some of those doing the damage are the so-called coyotes, those who are profiting from trade in illegals and furnishing them to job sites for work. Others are the cartels and their mules bringing drugs to the United States. All of the stories are heart rending. I have read memorials to Americans killed in the line of this battle of invading forces that like locusts devour everything in their path.

The most extreme case besides aliens killing Americans occurred in Arizona where illegal were stopped at gunpoint on a ranch and then sued for violation of their rights and won the ranch. This cannot be America, can it? This is not who we are? This is war and all we do is sit and watch Congress wring its hands and then give more tribute in the form of gifts to the invaders.

Below is the posting in January 2019 of one I read by Melissa Peters.

Catarina, Tx 1/17/2019

In the last 3 days, we have had 2 major bailouts on our ranch. They both involved coyote haulers using stolen vehicles out of San Antonio. The first one tried to ram down our main padlocked gate, but then busted through a pasture fence when agents were hot on their tail. The second vehicle ended up crashing through our neighbor's fence after they attempted to bust through ours.

This is happening EVERY single day down in South Texas and the ranchers are left to pay for the damage. I wish the rest of the United States could come down and see that this has turned into a full-fledged cartel business. If you don't know the details of how all of this works, let me map it out for you......

> *1. The cartel has complete control of the Rio Grande River (our Tx border) and they charge EVERY single illegal immigrant a minimum of $5,000 to cross the river.*
> *2. Once they cross, they travel through OUR ranch land / cities to make it to their destination. A lot of the women are raped as they prepare to cross.*
> *3. There are usually people on the US side (illegals and citizens) that get paid to pick up drug loads and or illegals. There's a lot of money at stake. If illegals don't pay full amount upon arrival , they are held in stash houses that are all over Texas!*

What part of this makes sense to anyone????

These illegals do not come with warning labels when we drive up on them being loaded into vehicles on our property. Our neighboring ranch foreman was shot at for driving up on an illegal exchange.

The other day we had up to 100 illegals from 6 different countries running through our property, we have driven up on dead bodies, our gate guards have been threatened, local schools have had to go into lockdown, windows have been broken, large groups hiding in brush, illegals sleeping in barns, and we can't leave the house without a gun by our side.

There are only a few of us to tell our stories. The coyote haulers are getting clever and are spray painting their trucks to look like oil field workers, so we have no idea who is on our property. Please listen to what's happening on our South Texas Border. How do we fix this? I bet I could ask a group of 3rd graders and they would have an answer for me tomorrow.

Please pray for our Border Patrol agents, because they are in the middle of this BIG political mess! It shouldn't be political, it's our country that's being invaded!!!! We have rules EVERYWHERE else that we go, why is this even acceptable? #frustrated[12]

Here is her Facebook posting as shared on November 3, 2018, in which she describes danger to her kids:

As we were making out afternoon round, a stolen vehicle out of San Antonio came plowing through our property/fence at a very high rate of speed. The vehicle was being chased by our amazing Border Patrol out of Laredo. Once the vehicle crashed, 10 plus illegals jumped out and started scattering all around us. My heart sank because my kids (ages 16 and 8) were in a separate jeep hunting at a nearby tank. The Border Patrol helicopter immediately came to the rescue."[13]

She further commented,

"We are not safe on our very own property. What if these guys would have encountered my kids during this bail out? Illegals back in the day would never bother us, but these young Zeta, tattooed, gang members are not all here for work. They are here to deliver back packs full of illegal drugs."[13]

I remember another posting in 2019 from a rancher's wife that six men came to the ranch house fence while her husband was away and shouted for her to bring them food. She made sure they saw she had a weapon, but when it got dark they started to attempt to sneak up. Fortunately her husband finally made it home and they called the Border Patrol.

A fourth posting I just saw on July 11, 2019 that there was a group of 40 Hondurans knocking on the door or a ranch house. A call to the Border Patrol was met with a quick response and they were rounded up. Here is the post I captured from Facebook:

> *Catherine Pearl Castaneda*
> *July 11 at 5:42 PM*
>
> *Well the day finally came, when the knock was on our door. To Tony's surprise 40 Hondurans. Thank you US Border Patrol for the quick response. You are so appreciated.*[14]

We are America. Even one incident like this is too much. One American death is too many. Any threats that we know can be prevented must be prevented. In my book, "*Gray Power Politics*," I included a picture from Facebook that was a memorial to a rancher killed by illegal aliens.

Border Ranch Wives Plea to Pelosi

In January 2019, wives of the Border Patrol issued a challenging letter to Nancy Pelosi (D), the Speaker of the House. Here is the full text of the letter:

Dear Ms. Pelosi-

> *"We the WIVES OF THE RGV (Rio Grande Valley) BP (Border Patrol) would like to cordially invite you to come visit McAllen, TX as President Trump did. It appears you are not busy today or any day, until Tuesday when you will return from your 4-day vacation. Since you've closed the House, you should come visit us!!*
> *Most of us wives will be home and available. We will not be grocery shopping, dropping off dry cleaning, taking our cars for oil changes, throwing our children birthday parties, or even jetting off to Puerto Rico for a few days. Heck, some of us didn't even sign our kids back up for activities b/c it appears you are unable or unwilling to negotiate. So, like I*

said, we'll be here!! We would like to show you around! You don't need to bring any security detail. Our husbands/boyfriends/fiancés/wives/significant others are actually very good at their jobs, thank goodness! And since you see no threat here, I'm sure you can just make a quick flight down here alone.

Hey, Trump might even allow you to use his plane for this visit!!

When you ask Trump to open the Government, then you'll negotiate, even though you already said you won't secure our border....this is kind of like when our kids want to eat dessert first, but they swear they'll eat their broccoli after...this is kind of like that, but no notes dumb enough to play that game!

For the record, many of us have saved for these days. We've faced many shutdowns before. But, we also recognize a weak leader when we see one, and we realize you may take awhile to come around.

We'd also appreciate if you'd stop pretending that you care about federal workers. If you did, you would care for their safety, not just their paychecks. We can hold out awhile longer, if it means our husbands and communities are safer.

You don't even need to worry about those MS-13 gang members you'll see running across the Border. Our guys and gals catch a lot of them. Like I said, they are good at their jobs!! I mean, if we had a wall we'd catch way more of them. But thanks to your laws, the ones we do catch we'll take to our huge air conditioned building, feed them, let them clean up, offering them clothes/hats/socks, maybe play on the billiard tables, or ping pong, or watch a movie, all while they wait for our charter bus to drive them to their "family" that lives in L.A. I mean, you don't need to worry about that...OMG I just realized...isn't L.A. part of your state?? Wow, sorry. My bad!

Also, it appears you do not own a pair of big girl pants. Do not worry, us BP wives own many pairs. In fact, that's all we own! We'd love to give you a pair of ours, you know we'd buy you your own, but we we're trying not to spend right now.

We look forward to seeing you soon!"[15]

Come on now those of you have any shred of decency, any of you who are empathetic to the plight of real Americans facing violence daily, Christians you profess sympathy for others, and just plain those of you who have common sense and can understand the daily pressures put on our own American citizens.

Build that wall! Build it high, deep and menacing. End the battle of Americans everywhere in this country who merely seek to pursue life, liberty, and happiness without the destruction of criminal aliens and drugs added to the mix.

CHAPTER 8

MORE ILLEGAL ALIEN ISSUES

I do not plan on directly covering all 54 of the issues posed by illegal aliens listed in Chapter 3, but indirectly I will continue to touch on most of them and certainly the important ones. The eight more issues with illegal aliens are added to the list of 54 issues, although in some ways they are treated under different names in the original list.

Allegiances

One has only to look at the flags of illegal alien demonstrators on national news and on social media to conclude illegal alien allegiance is not to the American flag or American values. Afterall, they have not studied for the citizenship exam, nor have they sworn allegiance to the United States of America. What other expectations should we have?

Entering illegally already pits the illegal alien against police, communities, organizations, Federal Marshals, (*los federales*) border patrol agents, authority figures, and the government in general. That makes it difficult to build allegiance to the United States.

I hate generalities; however, if the majority of cases fit, I will gladly use them. The only thing they want is American money and resources. They do not care for the environment, for the American worker, or for anyone in society, except for themselves. It really matters little if a few or a majority engage in crime. It matters even less is the majority are good people. What does matter is the terrible cost to Americans in money, wages, medical damages and all the rest of the items on the list. If they were legal entrants to America, we would have at least some assurance most of these things would not be a problem.

Assimilation

Assimilation, in the sociological sense, is the process of acceptance, absorption and integration by a people or person into the culture and ways of doing things of another society or culture. I often prefer the word for this process as being "enculturation." This includes transfer of allegiances, education into the history, tenets, belief systems, political processes, skill acquisition for survival in the new context, and economic adaptation.

Tolerant societies and cultures like the United States allow for ethnic differences, racial mixture and fascination with heritage, but with the understanding that acceptance means peaceful integration and exchange of ideas.

Assimilation into the American fabric is a long slow process for those who enter illegally. They attempt to use their own language as much as they can to live in the United States. Being the witting host to them means bending over backwards. We all know what can happen when you bend over backwards!

Failure to assimilate increases the burden on every citizen of a country. Understanding is the first victim.

Coddled by do-gooders, unscrupulous employers, misguided and un-American politicians merely for their votes, and continued illegal practices they once pursued in their own country against authority lessens their urgency for assimilation.

Illegal aliens have no basis for understanding the new culture and methods of assimilation with what is basically expected of them. It is rather like taking a cowboy to a Manhattan debutante ball without giving instructions on what to wear, how to be polite, and how to dress properly for the occasion.

Difficulties of assimilation are not just for those who come to the United States illegally, but those who refuse to give up old ways, old concepts, or who attempt to force their will on their new culture of residence, rather than adapting to the new one.

Assimilation into American culture is characterized by acceptance and practice of the following basic series of cultural characteristics:

- Acceptance of the U.S. Constitution as the bedrock for laws.
- Learning and understanding the laws of the new residence.
- Learning rights and duties of good citizenship.
- Liberty to pursue a dream within the confines of culture.
- Learning how to be happy in the new environment.
- Respect for police, military and first responders.
- Respect for authority.
- Respect for the flag and how to show it.
- Standing for the flag and national anthem.
- Understanding the issues of a political campaign.
- Voting without coercion.
- Work ethic, meaning willingness to find and go to work.

Illegal aliens miss the basic processes and learning experiences that a legal immigrant must go through and learn to become an American citizen. Becoming a citizen through naturalization is a process in which a non-U.S. citizen voluntarily becomes an American citizen. U.S. citizens owe their allegiance to the United States and are entitled to its protection and to exercise their rights and responsibilities as citizens.[1]

To become a U.S. citizen, you must:

- Have had a Permanent Resident (Green) Card for at least five years, or for at least three years if you're filing as the spouse of a U.S. citizen
- If you apply for naturalization less than six months before your Permanent Resident Card expires, or do not apply for naturalization until your card has already expired, you must renew your card.
- You can apply for naturalization before you receive your new Green Card, but you'll need to submit a photocopy of the receipt of your Form I-90, Application to Replace Permanent Resident Card, when you receive it.
- Meet certain eligibility requirements including being
- At least 18 years old at the time of filing
- Able to read, write, and speak basic English
- A person of good moral character
- Go through the ten-step naturalization process which includes
- Determining your eligibility to become an American citizen
- Preparing and submitting form N-400, the application for naturalization
- Taking the U.S. Naturalization Test and having a personal interview
- Ceremony before an immigration judge with an oath of allegiance.[2]

That is a lot to be missed. The checking of the applications is not only important, but essential to exclude terrorists and unsavory character characters with willful intent to rape, pillage, and murder American citizens.

American citizens have the right to expect exclusion of criminals and potential criminals. That is a duty we ascribe to government and includes the rock bottom requirement of national defense. How can people not understand the importance of collecting information on who is coming to America and why they are here, then separating the potentially good citizen from the certain bad ones?

Education

Refer to Chapter 3 for the massive cost of educating illegal alien children. Consider my own list here for the tremendous costs of educating children:

- Teachers
- Facilities
- English as a Second Language Specialists
- Buses and transportation

The cost is in the billions of dollars and it continues to escalate every year with the heavier increase, particularly since 2016.

We are talking the waste of billions by the states and federal government just for these categories. Then add in the new impetus of billions more in scholarships that unconscionably are now proposed and being given to these illegal aliens.

When I am writing of education in this chapter, though, I am writing about adult education. Illiteracy begets ignorance and ignorance or incapacity to learn begets illiteracy. Illiteracy is excluded in the proper processing of immigrants who applied legally to enter the United States. A large segment of illegal aliens is not literate in their own language in their own country of origin. Now they are in another culture that they understand even less. Consider the discrepancy in understanding everything from the laws of the United States to the meaning of words and phrases.

Ignorance leads to manipulation by those who wish to use and abuse the illegal aliens. Political party bosses salivate at the ability to get them to vote in the United States, despite the illegality of doing so. Organizations that specialize in protesting has a group immediately available that they can pay to protest even violently when wanted to do. Crimes go unreported for fear of revealing their status in society.

Language Disruption

Since illegals are not tested for rudimentary English language capability, everything from earning a driver license to understanding basic laws and signs is a challenge both to them and to the safety and security of American citizens. They become the chaos in our country.

Morality

Illegal means illegal and illegal aliens already broke the moral code of humankind. Without the proper vetting through checks in the country of origin, there is no way to assume moral turpitude of any of them.

Political Views

When welfare is the only political view and when one political party seems to offer both that and non-prosecution, there is no contest as what political views they might have. Operating purely in self-interest and self-perpetuation, they will support whoever offers them the sweetest deal, whether or not it is at great cost to the entire taxpayer base.

Socialism/Communism

Socialism and even communism is acceptable in many societies and countries. Such attitudes are counter to American culture and politics increasing the dangers presented by illegal aliens unenculturated. The majority of these aliens has no basis for decision making on the subject of socialism versus the free enterprise system and thus advocate for all the free stuff they can get.

Ungratefulness

I understand that the prospect of deportation, or being deported does not endear America to the illegal aliens, yet they have the wish to remain. That does influence voting patterns, lead to riots and other forms of violence, and to bad-mouthing the host benefactor country.

CHAPTER 9

RETURN TO SANITY

I commend the federal government for coming up with the coolest acronym possible, ICE. Customs enforcement was the perfect addition to the name Immigration and Customs Enforcement Agency (ICE).

When I was in the military, a person I knew was assigned as a Colonel to Secretary of State, Henry Kissinger. There was a crisis that arose and Kissinger asked him for all the options that he could think of to be listed in order of feasibility and priority. As I recall the crisis had to do with the English and Argentinians over the Falkland Islands. The Colonel thought for a day and prepared a list. When he handed it to Kissinger, Mr. Kissinger said, "The list is not complete." The Colonel was taken aback. His list was extensive and included military intervention options. Kissinger said, "You left out use of nuclear weapons and nuclear war."

The Colonel was aghast! "But Britain and Argentina are friends of ours," he responded. Mr. Kissinger said, "I want all options and then you tell me what we should or should not do. The list must be complete." My friend never forgot the lesson and when told to me neither did I. Consequently, I am listing some options I can think of for dealing with illegal aliens. It is up to the policy makers to sort them out.

The first ten options are feasible and all of them should be considered viable things to do. Not just one, but a series of measures is needed to resolve the problem and the issues. The second set is less feasible on the spectrum of possibilities, but they are doable. The first two are high visibility projects that not only are under consideration, but are somewhere in the process of being implemented with some members of Congress digging in their heels for no apparent and kicking and crying crocodile tears over the plight of the illegal aliens.

Projects for Immediate Implementation

Build the Border Wall

There are about as many images and theories on building the border wall as there are companies and engineers. My vision for a border wall as an obstacle stems from my background in military intelligence. My thoughts immediately ran to Normandy style fences and tank obstacles, claymore mines at the base or on the wall, sensor technology to provide alerts to border monitoring posts, wall guards in high towers that can cover half the distance to the next post, electrification, and land minefields to canalize the enemy.

Facts

Border Distance. While the precise distance from Brownsville, Texas to San Diego, California is 1,954 miles, the distance is only one-sixth that of the Great Wall of China, most of which has lasted for 2,000 years.[1]

Distance to be covered. As The Guardian reported from a conversation with Donald Trump on Air Force One flying to Paris, Trump does not believe the border wall must stretch the entire distance, but less than half the distance at about 900 miles of barriers. President Trump cited mountains that are difficult to scale, rivers that are uncrossable, remote desert on both sides of the border, and other natural barriers that prevent or slow down human and vehicular traffic.[2]

Specifications. The specifications called for 30-foot high plain concrete wall or walls of a combination of materials "other than concrete," in order to leave the playing field open and allow contractors to be creative in the process. Anti-tunneling provisions are include at least six feet underground to prevent the tunnels that drug lords have used in various border locations. "Border Patrol officials would not provide any details about what the barriers looked like below the surface, saying only that many went 'well beyond' the six-foot minimum."[3]

Included in the specifications are that the wall-barrier "must be able to withstand at least 30 minutes of force from a sledgehammer, car jack, pick axe, cutting tools, oxy/acetylene torch or other similar hand-held tools."[4]

This excludes easy to cut materials such as hollow pipe, or steel in columns with a gap between the columns. Hollow steel pipe a half inch thick could be cut though in under an hour and steel is malleable enough that it could easily make an opening in a wall by small equipment. Steel also rusts.

Border patrol officials have repeatedly said that they want to construct a wall that would be effectively impossible to scale — that it should be "physically imposing," measure between 18 and 30 feet high and include "anti-climbing features."[5]

Many of the contractors added a rounded tube at the top of their prototypes; they believe it will make it far less likely that anyone could reach the top. "It makes it impossible to straddle or use to get a rope ladder across because there is nothing to hook onto," Deputy Chief Patrol Agent Roy D. Villareal said.[6]

Plans

Research of wall construction plans was very interesting. Many questions have to be answered in advance of construction regarding the purposes, acceptable costs per segment, materials that withstand challenges of the environment like weathering and invaders human efforts to defeat it, technology built into the wall or supplemental to it, aesthetics on the U.S. side only or both sides, and visibility issues through the wall to ascertain the threats posed by wall-breachers,

The best source I found was an article from 2017 in the New York Times that reported on eight (8) prototypes in the San Diego area that were being studied at the time. The article concluded that for different sectors of the wall, different building techniques would be required. For example, the wall through urban terrain may of necessity be different from that in remote desert environments.[7]

Purposes

To the casual observer there is only on purpose. That purpose is to stop the flow of illegal aliens into the United States. Certainly that is the overriding objective and mission of a border wall, but the real questions become what do you want to do to them and the best way to accomplish that feat.

Think creatively with me for a minute. Do you want them to be temporarily stunned and disabled, injured by attempts to breach the wall, impaled by the wall, dead?

Cost to Build

What is the acceptable cost, or does that really matter, since a $10 billion wall produces a $130 billion annual reduction in economic and social costs plus saves lives and property while cutting down the flow of drugs and gangs?

The contractors that built the eight prototypes were six companies. W.G. Yates & Sons and Caddell Construction had two different protypes with different materials in each of them. ELTA North America is the Israeli firm that built their own wall for control of a portion of their border. The other three were Texas Sterling Construction, KWR Construction and Fisher Sand & Gravel. Cost is less of a factor in the evaluation, than performance and durability. The range of cost was from a low of $320,000 per segment to $470,000.[8]

Materials

The prototypes presented the government with a number of material choices. Among the materials were concrete, steel and brick with built-in enhancers like barbed wire and technology such as acoustic and visual sensors. Then the choices further reflected things like partial ability to see through the wall by spacing beams or tubes, aesthetics that responded to the word of Trump to make it a big fat beautiful wall, and different materials for each of the two sides.

Technology Built into the Wall

Some feel that mixed-material walls have a better chance of having more technological capabilities. These smart walls could incorporate radar, acoustics and other types of surveillance embedded in the infrastructure. One of the contractors bidding on the wall is ELTA North America, an Israeli defense contractor that specializes in radar and communication equipment.

"My sense is they will select multiple awards for these types of infrastructure," said Jayson Ahern, a former acting commissioner of Customs and Border Protection who was involved in the construction of a border fence during the George W. Bush administration. "Some will be for technology, some for when they just need a wall."[9]

This means that there are anticipated future add-ons to the wall building project involving placing and implementing technology. I believe that is a necessity along with continued human reaction teams and officer.

Aesthetics

When President Trump proclaimed the wall would be "Big" and "Beautiful," contractors considered everything from murals to paint patterns. "The only wall that actually has a brick facade is the prototype from Texas Sterling Construction. But in keeping with the guidelines, the pattern appears only on the U.S.-facing side. What Mexico gets to see is a bare concrete wall lined with barbed wire."[10]

Transparency

Border Patrol Officers clearly prefer a wall though which they can see and identify threats to wall integrity. Viewing the threat is an adjunct of the capability for rapid response to a projected wall incursion. This is especially important in the densely populated urban areas like Tijuana and San Diego, Nogales and Nogales, Ciudad Juarez and El Paso.[11]

Environmental Considerations

There are four environmental challenges posed by the nature of the wall to be built. In some cases variants of the wall to make it lighter or less solid, are examples that must be considered. The four primary challenges are sustainability from weathering and repeated attacks to the structural integrity, hydrology and the flow of water, earthquake fault lines, and impact on wildlife and their habitats.

Sustainability. Weathering such as rust on steel poses one sustainability challenge. From my historical perspective, the Golden Gate Bridge in California is a model of sustainability and survivability for a steel-paneled structure. Concrete and brick would not suffer as much from weathering, but may be less feasible. I presume the mud, mortar and rock of the Great Wall of China are not under present consideration, although 2,000 years works for me.

Hydrology. Obviously river flows and aquifers are important elements of the discussion. No doubt areas of the wall must make allowances for hydrology leaving gaps for water flow purposes. As long as that is envisioned and planned for, it simply means Border Patrol concentrations need to be on those gaps, which I call canalization from my military background in which invaders are forced to squeeze in and through a confined space protected by means other than a barrier or obstacle.

Earthquake Survivability. In an earthquake the lighter the fence, the better off it may be. Connectivity between panels or segments may be important to limiting the damage. That would mean providing ways for the wall to separate during an earthquake and not affect major portions of the rest of the wall on either side. As one structural engineer who inspected the current 650 miles for border fence emplacement, as mandated by the 2006 Secure Fence Act, said, "every mile of the southern border had to be carefully inspected."[12]

Wildlife. Mating patterns like those of wild burros are being taken into account in the border inspection process. Birds and insects presumably have no problems flying over the wall. Border wall proponents believe the impact on wildlife will be small and environmental concerns easily waived. Environmental activists see the wall as another governmental program endangering wildlife.

The truth may lie somewhere between. In fact some species might be enhanced by a border wall, just like marine life are enhanced by sunken boats.

Monitor and Maintain the Wall

Building the wall is only half the battle. Monitoring and maintaining the wall then becomes paramount. As Robert Frost said in his poem, "Mending Wall," "Something there is that does not love a wall."

The wall is not the be-all and end-all of border security, nor is it one easy solution, although it goes a long way to eliminate the threat of illegal aliens. It is one element of border security, but only part of the solution. Furthermore once built, it there for a longtime without further structural costs, depending on who tries to the breach the wall and how.

A border wall must be monitored and maintained for it to be effective. There are active and passive forms of monitoring a wall.

The active measures are patrols of the border by humans and trained dogs or other animals, active sensors like robots and daily flying of drones along the border wall.

Passive measures that could be included are motion censors, closed circuit television cameras, warning sounds or shots, moats, minefields, razor wire and electrification.

Deportation with Prejudice

Don't anyone get excited about the use of the word prejudice. This is the legal term usage that means a court action is taken against an individual regardless of color or ethnicity. Deportation with prejudice is already being used, certainly in criminal cases and other heinous acts and should be applied to any illegal alien found in the United States with the provision that none of them can ever enter the United

States again without stronger punishment. In essence they are exiled, or banished.

Voter Fraud Prevention

Despite fact checking organizations to the contrary, America is experiencing massive fraud in voter registration and election voting by illegal aliens who are rounded up and told to vote and how to vote by their Democratic benefactors who are their co-conspirators. Elsewhere, I pointed out it is a simple step to check a box on a driver license form stating one's eligibility to vote and directing that state to send them registration documents and ballots.

National ID cards can supplant driver licenses as an identification document. ICE agents can swarm the polls at election time. Citizens could purchase an ICE logo jacket, or one with ICE in big letters on the back as a deterrent. It might be easier to just purchase a blue jacket and have the logo or the printing pasted on the back and front.

Comprehensive databases can be accessed nationwide on election day to validate the right to vote. In the digital computer age, that should be a cinch.

States like Texas have pressed other measures for identification purposes, but largely have been cancelled out by the Supreme Court. That must change in the future and the courts must understand the gravity of not having solid evidence of the right to vote. Illegal voter fraud a grave threat to the integrity of the United States.

National Identification Card Establishment

Previous efforts to establish a National Identification Card (NIC) have all been attacked by both the left and right sides of the political spectrum. Americans in general have long had a hate relationship with the idea stemming from such systems being implemented in totalitarian countries in the past, especially Nazi Germany and Communist Russia.

My thought now is, why the concern? It certainly can assist in citizen identification at a time when it becomes more imperative for things like voter identification now that driver licenses have been compromised by states like California. We already have a de facto NIC with Social Security cards. There is only one step needed and that is a super card that cannot be compromised or duplicated and containing fraud prevention technology. It can be additive as a second form of personal identification, or incorporate the social security number. For my money I suggest a separate card so as not to compromise the social security number.

The liberal ACLU contends there are five reasons for not having such a system, all of which are easily refuted in the computer and digital age.[13]

Reason #1: A national ID card system would not solve the problem that is inspiring it.

While they admit digital fingerprints and other technology can be used, they point to the potential for carriers to obtain fraudulent documents under any circumstances and cannot believe a system can be created to make identification foolproof. They further point out that cost, according to the Social Security Administration that sends out their cards would be at least $4 billion. As they put it, "It is an impractical and ineffective proposal - a simplistic and naïve attempt to use gee-whiz technology to solve complex social and economic problems."[14]

Reason #2: An ID card system will lead to a slippery slope of surveillance and monitoring of citizens.

The ACLU contends a national ID card system would create an internal passport significantly diminishing freedom and privacy of citizens.

This is a concept that I now charge the ACLU with being naïve. Government has complete digital controls at their disposal anyway for tracking citizens and intervening in their privacy including GPS on cellphones. A National ID card would **not** significantly add more opportunities for control.

Reason #3: A national ID card system would require creation of a database of all Americans.

Really? Now I am laughing at the ACLU. Databases? That has never stopped the government from obtaining information, though by a longer process. Let us consider government and nongovernmental databases. A simple list will do.

Governmental Databases
- Social Security
- Internal Revenue
- Military Records
- Federal and State Retirement Records
- Department of Motor Vehicle Registration Records by state
- Criminal Records
- Court Filings
- US Postal Service Address Records

Nongovernmental Databases for Access
- Telephone Records including White and Yellow Pages
- Social Media including Google, Facebook, Instagram, and Twitter among others
- Credit Cards including Discover, Visa, Mastercard, and American Express
- Employment Records
- Cellphones with GPS

- Credit Reports

This list is not exhaustive, yet pervasive and available. Who are they kidding? Probably themselves. They go on to list minutia such as what if they are stolen, what proof is required to get one, records could contain errors, the database could be expanded and government agencies would soon link into it. These are all the usual "what ifs," and are simply throwing out red herrings to distract lawmakers.

Reason #4: ID cards would function as "internal passports" that monitor citizens' movements.

So? The ACLU goes on to worry about them being used pervasively and being recorded and monitored as internal passports. My point is that already happens. There is no difference in their claim and present reality without the card.

Reason #5: ID cards would foster new forms of discrimination and harassment.

The ACLU contends it would "foster" discrimination and harassment of anyone perceived as looking or sounding foreign. Then they turn around and say that already happened with previous Immigration Acts. Again, I question what is the difference between that and having the card. In fact, the card would less to less length discrimination and harassment.

2. Driver Licenses

Comparing the place of record, date of birth, picture, and other information can be provided by the DMV and can be ascertained when presented at the request of authorities.

Driver Licenses are now compromised for identification purposes at the ballot box by states such as California that now grant them to anybody applying for one, whether legally there or not. That ruins presentation for voting. In fact in many if not most states there is simply a box to check if one wishes to register to vote and the driver license acts are the purveyor of that right.

3. Marriage Licenses

Marriage license records should include place of marriage and names of father and mothers.

4. Birth Records

Obviously this is the basic document of greatest importance. Authenticity must be established and compared with place of birth and parents' names. Computers can check these records with state archives almost instantly. They are the key to identifying and catching illegal aliens and of preventing voter fraud.

5. Remittance Tracking to Foreign Destinations

When money is sent to foreign relatives and banks it can be traced. Records can be mandated to go through a central set of computers for informational comparative purposes.

No Welfare Reception

Word has spread that if one can get into America and hide, they can receive welfare in dollar amounts that are a magnet to the citizens of poor countries in Africa and South America. I can see their discussions now. Go to America. Apply for welfare and live the rest of your life like a king, or queen.

Insuring there is no support system will either make

them adjust to their new environment, or scurry back to their old one. We must take away any incentives for coming to the United States by increasing the obstacles and cutting off the rewards.

Only Emergency Medical Aid and Assistance

There is still a heavy burden on taxpayers with providing medical aid and assistance. The sooner the aliens are extracted from the U.S., the less the cost will be. Deportation should be an urgent affair and not one sullied by court cases.

No Birth Right to Remain in the U.S.

Most countries of the world practice jus sanguinis, which is birthright by blood of one or both parents. All 190 countries use this standard for granting citizenship. Then there is jus soli, which is an added factor for citizenship.

Of the current list of 190 countries of the world, only 33 allow birth on their soil as providing automatic citizenship. 29 of the 33 are in the Western Hemisphere. That is 16% of the countries of the world practice jus soli, which is citizenship by birth of anyone in the country. That makes pregnant illegal aliens hurry to run into the U.S., since the incentive is birthright and all the attendant money that comes with that factor.

Deferred Action for Childhood Arrivals (DACA) is for children born of parents who are not U.S. citizens, but nevertheless, have their children on U.S. soil, thereby granting them automatic citizenship. These children are called "anchor babies," since it gives the foreign and often illegal aliens a foot in the door to their own stay in country. The propaganda name is, "Dreamers." They are presently a highly contentious issue in domestic politics and have been so since the introduction of the program in 2012. They are all presently in limbo still in 2019.

The U.S. Citizenship and Immigration Services under the Department of Homeland Security were directed under the Obama Administration to establish guidelines for processing DACA children for citizenship. The age criteria was the program was for anyone under the age of 31 as of June 15, 2012.[15]

The current status of DACA, as of July 19, 2019 is that the program is still in limbo , since the Trump Administration had issue with the process of accepting the nearly 700,000 that fall under the undocumented program. This status will continue likely into the election year of 2020, since the US Supreme Court decided not to act on the effort of the administration to end the DACA program, meaning there will be no action until then. Lower court rulings blocked the Trump effort to end it, but it remains for the Supreme Court to decide the issue.[16]

As reported in Education Week, "The Supreme Court's move comes just a few days after Trump suggested that the Dreamers' fate could be linked to his demand for $5.7 billion to fund a wall along the U.S.-Mexico border. The money would come as part of an agreement to end the month-long partial government shutdown. In exchange for the wall funding, Trump offered three years of protections for Dreamers, as well as for holders of temporary protected status, a program that allows immigrants from countries in crisis to live and work in the United States legally. But congressional Democrats dismissed Trump's latest offer, in part because the deal didn't offer a path to citizenship for the Dreamers."[17]

A potential decision will have a major impact one way or the other. Besides the students many of whom have graduated, there are about 9,000 undocumented DACA protected teachers working in U.S. schools.[18]

Citizenship Question on All Decennial Census Forms

Talk about contentious political issues such as building a bridge and there is another highly controversial dispute in 2019 over placing the question of citizenship on all census forms for the 2020 census. The chapter in this book dealt with the citizenship question issue.

Comparative Computer Tracking

The ability of a government at any level to cross compare information is extensive. Many would say intrusive, but in the case of identifying illegal aliens highly constructive and invaluable. I thought of at least eight records of major use and importance for such a project. Many of them I remember being used for military intelligence background checks and information.

1. IRS Forms

IRS forms are a great place to start. Tracking of financial information, address, employment of record and social security number must already be coordinated.

6. Workplace Records

Workplaces must keep a good set of employee files for everything from emergency contacts to alternate phones and where education and training in life took place.

7. Financial Records

Bank financial records can be compared with transfers of money to foreign banks and cross compared with other records to establish residences and contacts.

8. Legal Documents and Proceedings

Court records are easy to acquire and compare the data. In fact there are advertisers online that claim they can access those records quickly. PACE is perhaps the one most used by attorneys to look up any records of trial proceedings or incarcerations.

9. Telephone Records

Both landlines and cell phones can be traced for usage and locational data. These can all be compared with likelihood of movement and associates.

10. Other Records

Everything from school records to military records can be included in this category.

At some point in time I believe the government will have massive databases for rapid comparison, if they do not even by this time. Not being an insider, I can still see the rapid ability to check records of everyone with any contact outside the home and even inside the home.

CHAPTER 10

IDEAS TO EXPLORE

The creative ideas in this chapter are mine. My recommendations for serious consideration are 1.) Bounties on the heads of illegal aliens and 2.) Formalized Citizen Posse units The acceptance of vigilante groups can be melded into the Citizen Posse organizations. The maintenance of inhospitable detention facilities is intended to remain a deterrent. The other two are thoughts that would be humanitarian nightmares, but I present them anyway just so everyone is aware of what might happen if things are allowed to continue. The ideas I brand unacceptable are: 1.) Poisoning of food and water caches and 2.) Turning them over to medical teams for scientific experimentation.

Bounty Offer

ICE could offer a bounty for reports leading to the deportation of illegal aliens. The value of each person deported in the short run (a year or two) would be in the 10's of thousands and over a longer period in the 100's of thousands (a few years). Bounties are not unreasonable and would encourage active roundups of illegal aliens.

I have several new thoughts on bounties. The bounties could include payments for law enforcement officials at state and local level half to the individual and half to the jurisdictional authority. This might be one way to break into sanctuary cities. There could be a bonus for the citizen doing the reporting.

Formalized Citizen Posse

A formalized citizen's posse with limited training and arrest authority could make a major difference. Here is my proposal for an organization that could include deployment to prevent border crossings, gather illegal aliens, and delivery of illegals to ICE agents:

STATE OF TEXAS INDEPENDENT RANGER UNIVERSAL POSSE (STIRUP)
Proposed by Roy E. Peterson

PREAMBLE

The State of Texas Independent Ranger Universal Posse (STIRUP) shall be organized with State of Texas acknowledgement and limited assistance including a state office, badges and credentials to serve in times of state crisis, state directed activities, and as a reserve for the State of Texas Rangers and as support for the Texas National Guard in fulfilling lawful missions approved by the Governor of Texas.

Supervision and control will be under the auspices of the Texas Rangers with one staff member designated as the responsible official for assigning missions, acquiring resources, county organizations, communications, and coordination with the Commander of the Texas Rangers.

The vision is to provide an augmenting force on ready call like the Minuteman Organizations in the Northeast of the United States, but with substantially more organization and control.

ACTIVITIES

1. Armed search for criminals.
2. Containment of protests through active and passive means.
3. Discovery and arrest of illegal immigrants including armed volunteer service along the Texas-Mexico border.
4. Ready call list for any potential or active shooter at a public school, college, or university in the State of Texas.
5. Intelligence collection on any illegal activities such as unauthorized sales of harmful substance drugs; discovery of illegal immigration aiders and abettors; observation and location of illegal activities; identification of any terrorist, terrorist organization, or potential terrorist threat; and any other activity deemed deleterious to public safety and lawful order in the State of Texas.
6. Logistical support including transportation of goods and services as requested by the governor.
7. Emergency assistance and relief in support of FEMA, Red Cross and other emergency organizations as requested.
8. Security for civic activities including political rallies, sporting events, or any other authorized event.
9. Sample events:

    A. Hunting armed, presumed armed, or potentially destructive and dangerous criminals.

    B. Protestors blocking roads and/or obstructing lawful activities of government officials or the public.

    C. Blocking illegal immigrants, finding illegal immigrants in the State of Texas, and assisting with the capture and detention of any illegal immigrants in any city, town, or county in Texas.

D. Observation and reporting of drug dealers, illegal substance sales, and manufacturing of illegal substances.

E. Hurricane and flood relief assistance as directed.

F. Observation and reporting of any terrorist activity or potential terrorist activity.

G. Response to any potential or reported active school shooting incident.

ORGANIZATION

1. An office and two person staff shall be provided at the State Capitol in Austin to serve as an action alert office, coordinator between the Governor and membership of STIRUP, and communications channel in times of crisis and emergency.

2. Each county in the State of Texas may have a volunteer STIRUP organization with priorities on activities occurring in their own counties.

3. The leadership shall be provided by one deputized officer named the Commander, and a second deputized officer, the Deputy Commander.

4. Office space will be requested with no payment. The office may be at the home of the Commander or Deputy Commander.

5. One volunteer officer will be assigned by the Commander to the County Staff as follows:

SP 1:   Membership and Personnel
SP 2:   Intelligence
SP 3:   Operations, Coordination, and Training
SP 4:   Logistics
SP 5:   Signals, Cyber Ops, and Information Processing
Assistance to the Deputy Staff members is to be determined by the Commander.

6. A STIRUP Organization Manual (STIRUP OM-1) shall be prepared to completely detail everything related to the

missions and operations of the STIRUP and lay out plans and operations.

MEMBERSHIP

1. Membership shall be voluntary and shall consist of former members who actively served in the military, police force, and emergency first responder organizations. Members shall be deputized under the organization of the Texas Rangers and lawfully operate as law enforcement officials with badges and credentials. The State of Texas will provide the badge and credential to each actively enrolled member volunteer.
2. Associate members may be accepted as volunteers and a plastic identity card provided; however, they only have normal citizen arrest authority and when practicable refer arrests to Deputies or the Texas Rangers.
    Class 1: Any individual with a valid State of Texas Hunting License.
    Class 2: All other armed citizens.
    Class 3: Unarmed citizens.
3. No one with a reported mental disorder including threats or abuse of any other person shall be admitted.

This is a serious proposal that could augment ICE, the Border Patrol and State resources. Liberal California and New Mexico would obviously not approve such an irregular force, but Texas and Arizona might.

Poisoning Water and Food Caches

An extreme measure would be to poison the water and food caches left by sympathetic illegal alien support groups in the deserts of the southwest. There are dozens of reports about such groups operating in those areas to provide what they regard as sustenance for those having crossed the border illegally.

Warning! Do not take this as a proposal, but as a cautionary image of what could happen when border ranchers are frustrated and angry, those who have lost family members to the illegal aliens who murdered them want revenge for their relatives, and other citizens interested in a more permanent solution and deterrent decide to take more extreme measures into their hands.

Scientific Guinea Pigs

Remember my purpose is to offer suggestions across the spectrum of actions from the mundane to the more stringent ones that thoughts allow. Even leaking a rumor that illegal aliens will be taken to a preserve and used for testing medicines, vaccines or other scientific endeavors can have a chilling effect when spread among Central American countries. I understand the hew and cry will relate to Nazi experiments, but why not use them for a productive purpose?

Vigilante Acceptance

While a formalized State Posse is being considered, there are vigilante groups that could have tacit or documented acceptance to conduct reconnaissance missions and detain for processing illegal aliens. These volunteer forces are committed and armed for the purpose of interdicting drug cartel members in particular.

ABC News presented a <u>Nightline</u> investigation of perhaps the best-known group, the Arizona Border Recon (AZBR) unit.[19] The report provided quotes by the leader of the group, Tim "Nailer" Foley about their operations and rationale that make a lot of sense. As reported by ABC, the recon unit was a heavily armed paramilitary force that is well organized and disciplined. They are not an authorized, sanctioned unit that critics say are dangerous, but admirers hope to emulate and praise. By nature and conduct, they are not authorized to do what they do, but this unit in particular is efficient and committed to the mission of stopping or at least interdicting illegal aliens.

While groups like the Southern Poverty Law Center label them extremists, Tim Foley considers themselves patriots contributing to society. In fact he said that since he lived in the area, it could be considered neighborhood watch. Andy Poliakoff, a New York Fire Department employee using his vacation to participate felt that although condemned by the Border Patrol, they secretly agreed with their recon effort. Another point was made that they actually saved lives and mentioned one alien who recently was in dire need of food and water that they helped by giving him those needed items. Foley shared a video with ABC News showing one of the illegal aliens who was exhausted an in need of water and food.[20]

With the ABC News team accompanying them in the Arizona desert, Foley said, "We believe there is a cartel scout watching our location just to our east. We're going to try to do a pinch on him. I got two headed south on this road and they're going to cut into the wash, and we're going to go to the top and push down."[21]

Although liberals hate the idea, the unit does not intend to shoot or abuse anyone. What they do is spot those crossing the border illegally. They chase them down, corral them and stay with them until the arrival of the Border Patrol or law enforcement. They have cameras planted along the main route used by drug mules and other aliens.

The AZBR leader, Tim Foley checks his volunteers by running background checks. "He doesn't allow drinking and routinely kicks our prospective members if they seem overeager and aggressive. Arizona ranchers are supportive of the unit. One of them stated, "They're doing what citizens out to do. They are helping the Border Patrol, helping all of us. We're in a foreign occupied area with the cartel scouts on our mountains."[22]

As ABC News reported, the illegal routes are natural trails through the desert carved by the heavy rains. The trails are littered with smuggling trade sings, empty black water bottles to prevent reflecting light, and abandoned carpet shoes used to strap under their shoes to not leave footprints.[23]

Foley has been accused of doing everything from planting IED devices to shooting the illegals, but he denied ever having done either and stated he has never been arrested for any form of misconduct.

The Arizona Border Recon unit is a perfect example of a group that could be given state paramilitary status under my plan for a state posse in each state that would operate with authorization as deputies to support law enforcement and border patrol units. It certainly worked in the old west and easily could work again. I plan on pitching this to the governors of at least Texas and New Mexico.

Inhospitable Border Reception Facilities

The Republican/Democratic party squabble reaches to accusations of inhospitable inadequate border facilities for processing illegal aliens who are caught in the process of invading the United States. A bill even passed the House of Representatives to provide millions for upgrades. The funny part is there were no complaints with the Democratic Party in control of the Presidency and now they are barking loudly with President Trump at the helm at the conditions and inadequacy of the situation. Trump inherited what is there. The Border Patrol is doing the best with what they have been allotted.

I provided a strong creative list of things to do to restore sanity to American culture and to the political process. The simple and most obvious thing to do is pass laws in accordance with some of the thoughts written in this book.

CHAPTER 11

TWELVE (12) PRINCIPLES WE MUST UNDERSTAND

If you do not recognize we have an illegal alien crisis, you would not recognize your own house burning down in front of your eyes and turning to ash. ~ Roy E. Peterson

Racism is not a Factor

The charge of racism related to eliminating illegal aliens in America and intent on coming here is one of the biggest lies we are told by leftists. Like other big lies, they hope that repeating it will make it true, but they are dastardly evil co-opters.

Far left revolutionaries have always adopted words that mean something to the majority, twisted them in their rhetoric to cover their agenda, and then castigates the opposition. Lenin was the master manipulator of word speak. He substituted the word "democracy" to cover totalitarian intentions when he claimed his communist party believed in "Democratic Centralism!" Guess how that one turned out.

Lenin found a way to claim his small minority party was the majority. Originally they were the Mensheviks, meaning minority. He then took on the name Bolsheviks, which means majority. There are dozens of words he subverted to paint his cause in a positive light regardless of the situation.

I see the same effort today to paint anyone illegal immigration as "racist." I categorically refute this assault on the logic and consciousness of good American citizens. My good Hispanic-American friends understand that just because a majority of illegals come from Mexico and Latin American countries, that does not mean being against them is a racial episode. Here is a point of logic: Since the majority of Hispanics in America rejects illegal immigration even from the country from which they or their relatives and ancestors came, those who call people against illegal immigration must include my friends and the majority of Hispanics.

I personally would not want illegal aliens of any color or ethnic group to feel free to invade our country. Another point of logic, in the future we could be inundated by illegal aliens from Russia, China, the Middle East and India in a short space of time. Ergo, this is not an issue for charging racist or racism.

American Labor Suffers Most

Illegal aliens ruin the wages of millions of American workers. If you really want to know who suffers most from the illegal alien invasion, it is the blue-collar workers whose jobs are taken. I do not understand how the labor union leadership has never dramatically opposed illegal immigration.

I understand back in history the need for braceros to work the California and Texas fields during World War II, when American manpower was scarce. That went away with the return of the soldiers looking for work and the continued invention of agricultural machinery and the production of those machines to effectively and efficiently replace some of the farm workers.

Wages suffer as much as American job loss. The far leftists in the United States want to boost wages to $15 per hour as a mandated wage for all. First, we know that would cost hundreds of thousands of jobs and part time employment. Second, we know that wages would already be higher in a fair competitive job market.

Understanding this simple point of logic is why so

many Democrats continue to move to the Republican Party. They fully understand what is happening and the false promises and pledges of the Democrats to be on the side of the working class both now and historically. Once upon a time and five decades ago they largely were correct in placing their faith in the Democratic Party. That faith vanished long ago, although some refuse to leave the party out of historical ties through their parents.

My father was such a case. He never voted Republican, because he was provided work under President Roosevelt to go to the Black Hills and construct everything from cabins to concrete benches and road rails. His employment by the Civilian Conservation Corps gave him the means to be on his own earning money and to send a pittance viewed as a major gift back to his parents working on farm near the mighty Missouri River.

I believe my father continued to vote Democratic up to President George Bush. Since Bush was considered a Texan by then, he hinted he voted for him on that basis. I know if he were still alive he would not only vote against the Democrats on the basis of their politics, but their beliefs.

I deserted the party though while in grade school in the 1950's after Truman. I was too young to vote, but I liked Truman as a President. If he were a candidate in a later era, I well could have voted for Harry. John F. Kennedy was the last Democratic President I respected and that was for his patriotism.

History

Illegal aliens are not the same thing as legal immigrants. There is a difference in kind. We must learn our history and that of the world to understand.

Having taught history and having had so many graduate courses in history, I believe everyone should have a thorough grounding both in history and American government as a requisite to graduate from high schools, colleges and universities.

History is where most of the leftists founder. Today's millennials cannot even differentiate between their ancestors who emigrated to the United States legally and the invasion of the body snatchers I call illegal aliens today. I hear the disconnect, "They all are immigrants, right!" Wrong! It really is comparing a sweet juicy apple to a rotten orange.

As I told you in other chapters of this book, a legal immigrant is processed through channels, checked for crimes and diseases, has a good background check, gets an interview and has documentation.

Illegal immigrants are like a drunk walking the rim of the Grand Canyon. Accidents are going to happen, meaning that we have not weeded out the criminals, terrorists, rapists, sex traffickers, and other anti-social personalities and kept them from destroying and corrupting American society and securing our own people from murders and other nefarious people bent on criminal activity.

Economics

Illegal aliens subvert the economy of a country. It is like paying tribute to a foreign conqueror.

I have already pointed out what they do to the labor market. I proved through facts and figures the tremendous cost to every taxpayer in the United States of subsidizing their illegal living.

Some do not understand that the billions in annual remittances become a drain on the resources of the country from which those funds are sent. There is a cost associated with that and again we are talking billions of dollars.

The high cost of welfare and supporting illegal aliens is a major contributor to the 22 trillion-dollar debt of our nation.

We cannot afford them under any circumstances, and certainly not for the sake of the economy.

Sovereignty

A nation that does not control its own territory and populace loses its sovereignty and control of its own destiny and becomes the colony of others and the world. ~Roy E. Peterson.

These words are pure logic. Sovereignty is something precious to be guarded by everyone in a society who is patriotic, believes in their country rightly or wrongly, wants their laws respected, and operates with liberty and freedom while in the pursuit of happiness. Anything else and they are at the whim of a controlling specter.

Voting Fraud Prevention

Allowing illegal aliens to vote is the ultimate act of incomprehensible suicide for any society or country. I issue a statement to Democratic Party leaders. Be careful what you wish for. You will go down with the ship of state and ruin the country, if you have not already done so.

I did not mince my words. I can tell by logic and observation when leftists begin to seize control of the hearts and mind of an organization and use that organizations to demand attention and furtherance of their unpatriotic and socialist agenda. I charge the party leaders with gross manipulation of the political environment, failure to perform their duty as American citizens, and un-American activities.

I am still moderate in making these charges. I am still logical and objective in my analysis. I call a spade a spade and a gravedigger a gravedigger. That is what you are.

Medical Damage

I predicted Americans would begin suffering diseases that once had been eradicated in our country. Unfortunately, I was right again. The chapter on medical costs and damages presented a prima facie case that any attorney would love to have in a court suit.

I believe most Americans can see the damages, but half of them are ignoring what has happened and what will continue to happen with illegal aliens stumbling across our borders with illnesses that formerly were the province of third world countries, not an advanced industrial power.

Our entire nation is at risk, yet obvious measures of prevention are not being taken due to an obstinate House of Representatives under the present Democratic regime. I trust enough Americans are tired of the rhetoric and racial dances of the left wing of the party, which now is most, and get to work to prevent illegal immigration as an emergency and by all means possible.

Good doctors can prescribe the medicine, but it is up to the patient to take it. The metaphor applies to our President and Congress with Trump being the doctor.

Uninsured Drivers

There is one mandate concerning uninsured drivers, protect our people and deliver them from the uninsured.

There is a high percentage of illegals now with driver licenses granted by California who do not have insurance. They are a menace on our roads as drivers and a cost to our own people in insurance rates that have to rise as a consequence.

This is one of the hidden costs of illegal aliens both in

terms of lives and in terms of money.

Violent Crime

Would you invite a criminal gang to come into your house by leaving an open door? No, you would not! Logic tells you bad things will happen.

Even one crime committed by illegal aliens is a tragedy and a travesty! Yet, our permissive legislatures both at the national and state levels permit it to happen DAILY. They are guilty and all should be charged with gross negligence.

Remember the old adage of an ounce of prevention! That saying has perfect logic behind it. We know the problem and we know one of the primary solutions, yet we **cavil** over doing nothing. Look up the word, "cavil." It means arguing over petty things. In this case it is a political potato that needs to be mashed.

American Citizens First and Foremost

Whatever happened to protecting our own? When did so many want to give away the farm?

I am a firm believer in taking care of our own first. We have abandoned that and hundreds of thousands of Americans from veterans, homeless, poor ghettos, and the general population that all could live better decent lives with the resources spent on foreigners.

Do you want people raised out of poverty? Do you want people to have sufficiency? Do you want people to all have a job? Do you want all people in society to have a home and a decent living? Then you must see the economic loss to the nation and the billions added to the national debt that must be paid down someday.

If I can see that, anybody can see that! Do not think you can take care of all? You are not doing that now.

Keep the Courts out of the Process

Illegal aliens have no rights except for the right to life and deportation.

This is not only logical, but expeditious. I know it will put a lot of attorneys out of business, but they can engage in their shady practices in other cases.

Again there are hidden costs about which I did not cover in my presentation chapters. Court costs, prosecutor costs, and individual costs must be exceptional and in the billions of dollars annually as well in the expansion of the court system to accommodate cases that should never be brought into a courtroom.

Humanitarian

A humanitarian, attempts to provide assistance to others. Taking in illegal aliens is not humanitarian. It is against humans from both our own country and those who are attracted by promises.

I am as great a humanitarian as anyone. I have given to the poor, helped the disabled, worked with kids, and have empathy for those still in need. I repaired toys for children for Christmas. I delivered food to the poor. I choose not to brag about it, but quietly go about my business and ways of contributing to others in society, but I will hanged if I believe in helping invaders.

Here is the crux of what you do not understand! A person living in a Central American country can earn a living at a level of wages or earning unfathomable to Americans. Many can live off the produce of the land for pennies on the dollar. When they come to America, their needs are elevated along with their expectations. Everything costs more. They need transportation to work, when they used to be able to walk a short distance to their job or endeavor in their country. They need better clothing to advance at their work or to do their job such as construction. They no longer have immediate access to things like bananas or pineapples and must pay so much more and go shopping for it.

I am just touching on a few items here, but having to get a car and not just a burro is a massive change for them. No one ever had to buy car insurance at their level in their third world country. No one had to purchase medical insurance.

You are doing no one a favor by allowing illegal alien immigration. Certainly not the alien and certainly not the American people.

One always must look at who benefits. They fall into the following categories;

1. Coyotes who sell their services.
2. Businesses who use and abuse them.
3. Drug cartels get their product cheaply transported.
4. Sex traffickers of all kinds of perversion.
5. Democrats who perceive more votes.

I leave you with this final stark reality! Now go think and vote!

ENDNOTES FOR ALL CHAPTERS

Chapter 1
Defining Immigration Notes

None

Chapter 2
Immigration History Notes

1. "Ellis Island United States Immigration." Maps of the World. https://www.mapsofworld.com/usa/facts-and-trivia/ellis -island-united-states-immigration.html

2. "History of Immigration to the United States." Wikipedia.

3. "First Australian Penal Colony Established." History.com. https://www.history.com/this-day-in-history/first-australian-penal-colony-established

4. Wikipedia. op. cit.

5. United States Constitution.

6. Wikipedia. op. cit.

7. Ibid.

8. Ibid.

9. U.S. Census Bureau.

10. Encyclopedia Britannica.

11. Wikipedia. op. cit.

12. Ibid.

13. Ibid.

14. Chy Lung v. Freeman. 92 U.S. 275 (1875) found in supreme.justia.com/ cases/ federal/us/92/275.

15. The Page Immigration Act of 1875. 43rd Congress, Session II, Chapter 141. 1875.

16. Chang, Kornel S. Pacific Connections. University of California Press, 2012, page 53.

17. "Immigration Act Passed over Wilson's Veto. " History.com. Accessed July 11, 2019/Updated June 14, 2019/Original February 9, 2010.

18. Zeidel, Robert F. Immigrants, Progressives and Exclusion Politics: The Dillingham Commission, 1900-1927. DeKalb: Northern Illinois University Press (2004).

19. "Immigration Act…" op. cit. Note 17.

20. Ibid.

21. Ibid.

22. Wikipedia. op. cit.

23. Zong, Jie and Batalovo, Jeanne. "Filipino Immigrants in the United States." Migration Information Source. March 14, 2018.

24. History.com

25. Ibid.

26. "Displaced Persons Act (1948)." Immigration History. The University of Texas at Austin, History Department, 2019. Accessed July 12, 2019.

27. Statistical Abstract of the United States, 1950.

28. "Displaced Persons Act (1950). Immigration History. The University of Texas at Austin, History Department, 2019. Accessed July 12, 2019.

29. "Internal Security Act (1950). Immigration History. The University of Texas at Austin, History Department, 2019. Accessed July 12, 2019.

30. "Displaced Persons Act (1953). Immigration History. The University of Texas at Austin, History Department, 2019. Accessed July 12, 2019.

31. "The Immigration and Nationality Act of 1952 (McCarran-Walter Act)." Office of the Historian, U.S. Department of State. Accessed July 12, 2019.

32. Ibid.

33. Ibid.

34. Ibid.

35. Ibid.

36. Glass, Andrew. "Eisenhower Signs Refugee Relief Act, August 7, 1953." Politico. August 7, 2018. (From "This Day in Presidential History by Paul Brandus.) Accessed July 13, 2019.

37. "Operation Wetback." <u>History.com</u>. https://www.history.com/news/operation-wetback-eisenhower-1954-deportation. Accessed July 13, 2019.

38. Coriden, Guy E. <u>Report on Hungarian Refugees</u>. Central Intelligence Agency. (Undated/Inferred date of September 1957) Declassified and approved for release 1994/Released July 1996. Accessed July 13, 201939.

39. <u>Wikipedia</u>. <u>op. cit.</u>

40. <u>Ibid.</u>

41. Pedraza, Sylvia. <u>Political Disaffection in Cuba's Revolution and Exodus</u>. Cambridge University Press. 2007, page 299.

42. "Immigration Reform and Control Act of 1986." S. 1200. 99th Congress. www. GovTrack.us, Accessed July 13, 2019.

43. <u>Wikipedia</u>. <u>op. cit.</u>

44. 8 USC 1158: Asylum (Text containing laws in effect July 12, 2019). From Title 8. Aliens and Nationality, Chapter 12: Immigration and Nationality Subchapter II-Immigration, Part I – Selection System. Accessed July 11, 2019. http://uscode.house.gov/view.xhtml?req=(title:8%20section: 1158%20edition:prelim)

Chapter 3
Undesirable Illegal Aliens Notes

1. "Problems with Illegal Immigration." Americans for Legal Immigration PAC. https://www.alipac.us/problems-with-illegal-immigration/

2. <u>Ibid.</u>

Chapter 4
Illegal Immigration Costs to America Notes

1. Blankley, Bethany. "Reports: Illegal immigrants receiving Medicaid costs taxpayers $18.5 billion annually. <u>Watchdog.org</u> Oct 19, 2018.

2. Richwine, Jason. "The Cost of Welfare Use by Immigrants and Native Households." <u>Cato Institute</u>. May 9, 2016. https://cis.org/Report/Cost-Welfare-Use-Immigrant-and-Native-Households

3. Johnson, Lance D. "Illegal Immigration Costs U.S. taxpayers $155 Billion per year (State and Federal)." <u>Natural News</u>. December 2018. Note the number came from the Federation for American Immigration Reform (FAIR).

4. Steven A. Camarota of FAIR wrote in an article on May 1, 2017, "Even Cato Agrees: A Border Wall Can Pay for Itself. https://cis.org/Camarota/Even-Cato-Agrees-Border-Wall-Can-Pay-Itself. Accessed February 27, 2019.

5. Camarota, Steven A. "Cato Flubs Illegal Immigrant Numbers When Criticizing President Trump." <u>Newsandtimes.com</u>. https://www.newsandtimes.com/politics/2017/07/, July 2017.

6. Camarota, Steven A. "Report: Welfare Use by Immigrant Households with Children. A Look at Cash, Medicaid, Housing, and Food Programs." <u>Center for Immigration Studies</u>. April 5. 2011.

7. Conover, Chris. "How American Citizens Finance $18.5 Billion in Healthcare for Unauthorized Immigrants." <u>Forbes.</u>

February 26, 2016. Accessed February 28, 2019. https://www.forbes.com/sites/theapothecary/2018/02/26/how-american-citizens-finance-health-care-for-undocumented-immigrants/#6361770b12c4.

8. Ibid.

9. Ibid.

10. Blankley, op. cit.

11. Ibid.

12. Ibid.

13. Ibid.

14. Ibid.

15. Ibid.

16. Bernal, Rafael and Lillis, Mike. "Remittances Play Huge Roll in Immigrant Economy." The Hill. October 31, 2016.

17. Morrison, Spencer P. "Remittances: Illegal Immigration's Hidden Tax." American Greatness. June 20, 2018.

18. DeSilver, Drew. "Remittances from Abroad are Major Economic Assets for Some Developing Countries." Pew Research Center, January 29, 2018. http://www.pewresearch.org/fact-tank/2018/01/29/remittances-from-abroad-are-major-economic-assets-for-some-developing-countries/.

19. Ibid.

20. Morrison. op. cit.

21. Ibid.

22. Ibid.

23. Ibid.

24. "Migration and Remittances: Recent Developments and Outlook" Migration and Development Brief 30. World Bank. December 2018.

25. "Migrants' Remittances to Mexico, Central America Jump to $53 Billion in 2018." Breitbart. January 2, 2019.

Chapter 5
Medical Costs of Illegal Aliens Notes

1. "The Dark Side of Illegal Immigration: Facts, Figures and Statistics on Illegal Immigration." http://www.usillegalaliens.com/impacts_of_illegal_immigra tion_Diseases. html.

2. "Six Diseases Return To US as Migration Advocates Celebrate 'World Refugee Day.'" Breitbart. June 19, 2016. https://www.breitbart.com/politics/2016/06/19/diseases-thought-eradicated-world-refugee-day/.

3. "Crisis of Seriously Ill Migrants Slams Border Patrol — TB, Pneumonia, Influenza, Parasites. Judicial Watch. Judical Watch Blog. Corruption Chronicles. January 7, 2019. Placed on social media. Camarota is Director of Research, Center for Immigration Studies."

Chapter 6
Illegal Aliens and Politics Notes

1. Cohn, D'Vera. "What to Know About the Citizenship Question the Census Bureau is Planning to Ask in 2020." Pew Research Organization. March 30, 2018.

2. Ibid.

3. Keith, Tamara. "Has Citizenship been a Standard Census Question?" FactCheck.org. March 27, 2018. (*NPR's* Hansi Lo Wang *contributed to this report.*)
https://www.npr.org/2018/03/27/597436512/fact-check-has-citizenship-been-a-standard-census-question, Updated on March 28, 2018.

4. Ibid.

5. Ibid.

6. "American Community Survey." U.S. Census Bureau. Accessed July 14, 2019. https://www.census.gov/programs-surveys/acs/

7. Ross, Wilbur, Secretary of Commerce, U.S. Department of Commerce. As quoted in Keith. Ibid.

8. Cohn. op. cit.

9. Ibid.

10. Ibid.

11. "Supreme Count weighs census question that could undercut California's Power," Los Angeles Times (via TNS), February 15, 2019 as reported by David G. Savage in the Daily Republic, Fairfield-Suisun, CA.)

12. Trump Tweet as quoted in Tottenberg, Nina. "Trump Threatens Census Delay After Supreme Court Leaves Citizenship Question Blocked." June 27, 2019.

13. Tottenberg, Nina. "Trump Threatens Census Delay After Supreme Court Leaves Citizenship Question Blocked." June 27, 2019.

14. Ibid.

15. Dinan, Stephen. "Court: Immigrants who vote illegally can be deported." The Washington Times. Monday, February 13, 2017. Accessed July 15, 2019.

16. Ibid.

17. Ibid.

Chapter 7
Crime and Illegal Aliens Notes

1. "New Research: The impact of illegal aliens on crime rates, data codebook and 'do file.'" The Crime Prevention Research Center. January 17, 2018.

2. Ibid.

3. "Criminal Alien Statistics." GAO-11-187, Government Accountability Office. March 2011.

4. Ibid.

5. Ibid.

6. "Criminal Alien Statistics." GAO-18-433, Government Accountability Office. Published July 17, 2018. Publicly Released August 16, 2018.

7. Ibid.

8. "Southeastern Provision Owner James Brantley Pleads Guilty to Federal Information." <u>Press Release</u>. The United States Attorney's Office, Eastern District of Tennessee. September 12, 2018.

9. <u>Ibid.</u>

10. <u>Ibid.</u>

11. <u>Judicial Watch</u>. NBC News Report. February 19, 2019.

12. #frustrated/Catarina Texas. <u>Facebook</u>. "Posting." Dated: January 17, 2019.

13. *#frustrated/Catarina Texas*. <u>Facebook</u>. "Posting." Dated: November 11, 2018.

14. *Catherine Pearl Castaneda.* <u>Facebook</u>. July 11, 2019 at 5:42 PM.

15. "Full Letter text – Border Patrol Wives to Nancy Pelosi." (My shortened title.) Text found on <u>The Daily Wire</u>. https://www.dailywire.com/news/42790/border-patrol-wives-have-proposal-nancy-pelosi-amanda-prestigiacomo

Chapter 8
More Illegal Alien Issues Notes

1. Usa.gov. https://www.usa.gov/become-us-citizen Accessed July 18. 2019.

2. <u>Ibid.</u>

Chapter 9
Return to Sanity Notes

1. Geraghty, Jim. "The Wall Is Being Built! (Slowly.)" National Review. June 29, 2018.
https://www.nationalreview.com/2018/06/us-mexico-border-wall-being-built-slowly/#slide-1

2. "Trump Says Mexico Doesn't Need to Cover the Whole Border." The Guardian (US Edition). July 13, 2017.
https://www.theguardian.com/us-news/2017/jul/13/mexico-border-wall-trump-plan-wont-need-full-border

3. Medina, Jennifer, Haner, Josh, Williams, Josh and Bui, Quoctrung. "Eight Ways to Build a Border Wall." New York Times. NOV. 8, 2017. Accessed July 19, 2019.
https://www.nytimes.com/interactive/2017/11/08/upshot/eight-ways-to-build-a-border-wall-prototypes-mexico.html

4. Ibid.

5. Ibid.

6. Ibid.

7. Ibid.

8. Ibid.

9. Ibid.

10. Ibid.

11. Ibid.

12. Ibid.

13. "5 Problems with National Identification Cards." ACLU. https://www.aclu.org/other/5-problems-national-id-cards Accessed July 19, 2019.

14. Ibid.

15. "Consideration of Deferred Action for Childhood Arrivals." U.S. Citizenship and Immigration Services. https://www.uscis.gov/archive/consideration-deferred-action-childhood-arrivals-daca Accessed on July 19, 2019.

16. Mitchell, Corey "DACA Status Update: In Place for Now, But Resolution Remains Elusive. Education Week. July 13, 2019. Accessed July 19 from http://blogs.edweek.org/edweek/learning-the-language/2019/01/daca_remains_in_place_for_now_.html

17. Ibid.

18. Ibid.

19. Karlinsky, Neal, Crawford, Shannon and Effron, Lauren. "Out on Patrol with Heavily Armed Civilian Vigilantes on Arizona's Border with Mexico." ABC News. February 1, 2017. https://abcnews.go.com/US/patrol-heavily-armed-civilian-vigilantes-arizonas-border-mexico/story?id=45201990

20. Ibid.

21. Ibid.

22. Ibid.

Chapters 4 and 5 are from my book, *Gray Power Politics. 2019.*

BIOGRAPHY OF ROY E. PETERSON
LTC, U.S. Army, Military Intelligence Retired

Photo: Captain Roy E. Peterson. Can Tho Vietnam, 1972.

LTC Roy Peterson served as an Assistant Army Attaché in Moscow during the peak of the Cold War Years from 1983-1985, as the first U.S. Foreign Commercial Officer in the Russian Far East for the U.S. Department of Commerce with dual duty as a Visa Issuing Officer for the U.S. Department of State, and as the first IBM Regional Manager, Vladivostok, Russian Far East (1993-1995).

He was Commander, Portal Monitoring, On-Site Inspection Agency in Votkinsk, Russia and Commander of the 5th Military Intelligence Company, 18th Military Intelligence Battalion, 66th Military Intelligence Group.

LTC Peterson was trained in Russian, German, and Vietnamese and used all three languages in their respective theaters of operation.

LTC Peterson is a recognized international trade and Russian political/military consultant. Roy was a recent faculty member with the University of Phoenix teaching global business, marketing, sales, management, military intelligence, unconventional warfare, and international trade.

Roy Peterson is a poet, songwriter, and award-winning bass voice singer.

Writing Credentials

LTC Peterson has had published more than 50 books, over 20 extensive secret intelligence studies, over 100 intelligence reports (unavailable), 2 MA theses, and 2 Institute publications. Throughout life he has written monographs, business proposals, and engaged in marketing, for which he has international credentials. He has written over 100 country, rock and gospel songs.

Military Intelligence Credentials

Analyst, National Security Agency
Phoenix Advisor MR IV Corps, The Delta, Vietnam.
Analyst, Defense Intelligence Agency.
Commander, Military Intelligence Company, Germany.
Manager, Army Security Clearances.
1st Army Staff Intelligence Advisor, Pentagon.
Selected to replace Ollie North on Security Council.
Presidential Rep. to Russia, On-Site Inspection Agency.
Army Attaché, Moscow.
Executive Officer, Intelligence Collection Unit
Honor Graduate, US Army Russian Institute.
Russian language fluency.
Human Intelligence Coordinator, 1st Gulf War.
Awarded Legion of Merit, Bronze Star.

Academic Credentials

BA, Hardin-Simmons, MA University of Arizona.
MA University of Southern California.
MBA University of Phoenix.
Ph.D., passed written and oral exams and remains ABD.
Defense Language Institute, Russian.
Graduate, U.S. Army Command and General Staff College.
Faculty Member, University of Phoenix.
Faculty Member, University of Maryland.
Faculty Member, University of Arizona.
Faculty Member, Western New Mexico University.
Faculty Member, Travel University International.
Graduate Assistant, American Government, Texas Tech.

Business Credentials

President, HPO International and TriCrown International.
VP, International Trade Company,.
VP, Investment Company.
VP and COO, Construction Development Company,.
VP Management Company.
Sold trucks to Russia.
1st USDOC Foreign Commercial Officer in Russian Far East.
1st IBM Manager in Russian Far East.
Taught International Trade and Global Business Management.
Director New Business Development for ENSCO.
Wrote operational and technical proposal for EG&G on
        Strategic Arms Limitation Talks Contract.
President Export Company.

BOOKS AND PUBLICATIONS AUTHORED
ROY E. PETERSON (82)

Poetry Books

A Child's Home Companion
All American New Holiday Classic Poems: 100 + Poems for Christmas…
Alien Inspired Verse: Poetry from the Universe
Alpen Splendor, Mountain Grandeur
Always Means Forever: Poetry So Clever Until the Twelfth of Never
America Needs Adult Advice
American Country Poetry: From the Prairie to the Parlor
American Classic Poetry: Poetry for the Majority
American Gold Classic Poetry: If it doesn't Rhyme
American Heartland: Poetry, Wit, and Wisdom
American Heritage Poetry Collection
American Patriot Salute
Angels All Around Us: A Great Garden of Verse
A Pink Moon in April: Poetry from the Periphery
As the World Burns: Poetry by the Fireside
Autumn Echoes: Poetic Treasure Trove…
Beauty Begets Emotion: Rhymes of Love and Devotion
Before I Go to Bed: Poetry for Dreaming
Between Darkness and Light
Beyond the Back Seat: Coming of Age Nostalgic Treat
Christian Poetry for the Heart and Soul
Classic Poetry Renaissance: Rhyme and Meter Make it Sweeter
Cultural Conservation Companion: Clever Poems for Smart Homes
Democratic Party Down the Rabbit Hole: Descent into Political Madness
Dreamers Dream While Poets Scheme: Poets Pursue the Theme
Eternal Spring: Poetry and Promise
Fables from the Funny Farm: Follies, Frolic, and Fun
Feet on the Ground: Heart in the Sky
For Love May Find You: Poetry with Passion
Grains of Sand: Poetry by the Sea
Guardian Angel: All My Tomorrows
Happy Haunting Halloween: Olde and New Classics
Harmony and Discord in an Atonal World: Revelations…..
Love is Made in Heaven/Romance is Made on Earth
Love That Lasts Eternally: Poetry of Romance and Mystery
McCamey Memories We All Share: Nostalgic Poems…
My Best Classic Poetry Collection: Arrows Sent in Your Direction
My Heart Has Not Forgotten: Where'er Thine Feet Have Trodden

Mystery Has an Accomplice: Poems You Won't Want to Miss
Out of the Shadows: My 110 Best Nature Poems
Poems for Happy Times Treasury: My Own Selected Best Classical Poetry
Poetry Knocking on the Door: Classic Rhymes
Poetry is Passion: Truth and Time in Classic Rhyme
Poetry When Nights are Stormy: Classic Poems to Warm the Heart
Race Relations Objective Perspective Poetry
Riveting Romantic Love Treasury: Vol 2 My Own Selected Best Classical Poetry
Songs from a Sultry Soul
Sonnets from the Inner Sanctum: Poetry for Posterity
Sonnets from the Mellow Breeze
Southern Comfort: New Classic Poetry from Me
Texas Stardust
Texas Trail Dust: Cowboy Campfire Collection
Treasury of Wit, Wisdom and Advice: Vol 3 My Own Selected Best Class. Poetry
What Lovely Ladies Desire: Classic Poems to Inspire
What the Heart Proposes: The Poet Discloses
Whither My Love: Treasury of Great Classical Love Poetry
When I Think of Heaven: Inspirational Sonnets, Soliloquies, Songs…
Where Love Dares to Go: Pathways Only Poets Know
Where the Foxes Play: Poetry to Read When the Fur Flies
While the Wind is Whispering Through the Sylvan Glen
Winter Casts Its Spell: Autumn Says Farewell

Poems Published by Prestigious Society of Classical Poets (22)

1. *July 4ᵗʰ Celebration, 2018* (July 4, 2018)
2. *The Poet's Soul with Artful Pen* (November 25, 2018)
3. *The Sordid Socialists and Cultish Communists* (November 25, 2018)
4. *The Commie Will Hijack a Word* (November 25, 2018)
5. *Where the Heart Goes* (April 13, 2019)
6. *In the Silence of the Evening* (April 13, 2019)
7. *If I Could Paint a Portrait* (April 13, 2019)
8. *Solemn Legion of the Brave* (May 27, 2019)
9. *May Old Glory Always Wave* (July 4, 2019)
10. *Veterans Day* (November 11, 2019)
11. *Why I Value Toilet Paper* (March 17, 2020)
12. *Planned Parenthood's a Euphemism (May 15, 2020)*
13. *Solemn Silent Soldiers Rest* (May 22, 2020)
14. *Hearts and Clouds* (January 14, 2021)
15. *Though Worlds May Die and Silent Be* (February 14, 2021)
16. *Lives There the Man* (March 14, 2021)
17. *Gun Control is Mind Control* (April 10, 2021)

18. *National Poetry Month Challenge: What is Poetry? Verses from my Poem, "Poets on Poetry," formed the basis for poets to write quatrains* (April 17, 2021)
19. *The Seven Dwarves of Old Age* (April 18, 2021)
20. *Epitaphs* (May 3, 2021)
21. *Living in a Purple Wood* (May 5, 2021)
22. *The Winds of War Now Howl (May 21, 2021)*
23. *Friends on the Wall* (May 31, 2021)
24. *The Future's Illumined By Deeds of the Past (July 4, 2021)*
25. *Memories of Memorial Day* is scheduled for May 2022.

Poems Published by Western Poetry
Writers of the Purple Sage (May 2013)
Tucson Sunday Morning (February 2014)

Poem Published by Hardin-Simmons University
"Night Storm." Quiet Thoughts. Hardin-Simmons University, 1963.

Special Accolades
Featured Writer, Society of Classical Poets. Journal VII, 2019.
Featured Writer, Society of Classical Poets. Journal VIII, 2020.
Featured Writer, Society of Classical Poets. Journal IX, 2021
Featured Writer, Western Writers, 2014.

History
American Attaché in the Moscow Maelstrom
Fight of the Phoenix
Soviet Intelligence Process (Out of Print Monograph)
The Velvethammer: Lieutenant Colonels Get Things Done

Historical Fiction
From Chapultepec to Castle Gap
Hitler's Secret Jet Designer: Jet Invention, Austrian Connection...
Iron Ikon: U.S. Foreign Commercial Officer Duty in the Russian Far East (Out of Print)
Russian Bears/American Affairs
Russian Romance: Danger and Daring (Out of Print)

Humor, Wit and Wisdom
Peterson Perspective: Humor, Wit and Wisdom

Juvenile
Albert: The Cat That Thought He Could Fly

Life Stories (Memoirs)

On the Edge of Night: Finding Love Again at 70 (Vol II Horny Toads Trilogy)
Pansy, The Texas Trapeze Artist
Paths Upon the Prairie
When Sunsets Glow: Finding Lost Love in Life's Afterglow (Vol III Horny Toads)
Where the Horny Toads Play (Vol I Horny Toads Trilogy)

Politics

American Made Crisis: Aliens in Our Midst
Demolishing the Demons: Theology and Politics Preparing for the New Crusade
*Gray Power Politics: Political Wants and Needs of the Newly Powerful Cross-cutting
        Demographic Segment*

Relationships

Magnetism to Marriage
Men and Divorce

Major Business Proposals

INF Treaty Portal Monitoring Proposal, On-Site Inspection Agency, 1991.
Victorville 442-Unit Apartment Complex, as Chief Operating Officer, 2003.

Three Masters Degree Theses

1. MA, Political Science, University of Arizona, 1969.
2. MA, International Relations, University of Southern California, 1970.
3. MBA, Global Business Management, University of Phoenix, 2001.

Music

First Prize: Platte Grade School Invitational Contest, South Dakota,
        4th, 5th and 6th grade Boy's Soprano 1952, 1953, 1954.
State of South Dakota All Grade School Choir.
First Prize: Tucson Arizona Country Music Festival, 1969.